# Conquest

# Conquest

## Or, A Piece of Jade

## Marie Stopes

MINT EDITIONS

*Conquest: Or, A Piece of Jade* was first published in 1917.

This edition published by Mint Editions 2021.

ISBN 9781513223070 | E-ISBN 9781513221571

Published by Mint Editions®

**MINT EDITIONS**
minteditionbooks.com

Publishing Director: Jennifer Newens
Design & Production: Rachel Lopez Metzger
Project Manager: Micaela Clark
Typesetting: Westchester Publishing Services

TIME: 1915.          PLACE: New Zealand and London

ACT I.
An Out-station on the Hyde's Sheep Farm, New Zealand.
Afternoon.

ACT II.
The Hyde's Homestead, New Zealand.
Morning.
Three or four months elapse between Acts I and II.

ACT III.
The Duchess of Rainshire's Drawing-room, London.
Evening.
About two months elapse between Acts II and III.

# Dramatis Personæ

*In the order of their appearance*:

First Shepherd.
Second Shepherd.
Gordon Hyde, *New Zealand Sheep Farmer*.
Roto, *an old Maori*.
Nora Lee, *A New Zealand Girl*.
Loveday Lewisham, *Nora's Cousin, out from England*.
Robert Hyde, *New Zealand Sheep Farmer, Gordon's Brother*.
John Varlie *alias* The Rev Dr. Chapman.
Recruiting Officer.
The Duchess of Rainshire.
A Cabinet Minister.
Smithers.

Also (*Without words*):

Two (Or Perhaps Three) Young Men *in New Zealand Khaki*.
Ladies and Gentlemen, *Guests at the Duchess' Evening Party*.
Maid, *Footman's substitute in uniform*.
Two Plain Clothes Officers.
One or Two Collie Dogs.
Sheep—One, Or More, *if convenient*.

# Act I

*The Scene is set in the hills of the sheep-raising part of the S. Island of New Zealand.*

*The back-cloth is painted with fine rocky and wooded hills and lakes, rather like Scotland but with a clearer, bluer sky and keener atmosphere.*

*The stage represents a temporary camp in a clearing, for the mustering and marking of sheep. There are boulders and groups of luxuriant trees. The grass is trampled under foot. Right Centre is an open fire with cooking utensils. Back Right the corner of sheep enclosures. On Left is a temporary cover, part canvas, part tree branches.*

*Two Shepherds are Discovered near the fire, binding up the leg of a sheep. The collie dogs prowl and lie around.*

1st Shep.: (*An old, wiry man*) A fine muster, this year.

2nd Shep.: (*A dour man, about 45 years old*) Aye.

1st Shep.: The best season I mind for ten years. (*Working with sheep's leg*) Plague take it, it's slipped. Lie still you bleatin' fule ye! And sheep s'd fetch a guid price this year and all.

2nd Shep.: Aye.

1st Shep.: I'm thinkin' these sheep will be making the fortune of the young masters, but they do nought but make work for us.

2nd Shep.: (*Spits*) Aye.

1st Shep.: The young masters must get an extra man, we never had to handle so many sheep.

2nd Shep.: Men'll be scarce now.

1st Shep.: They will that. Do you hear they recruitin' fellows are scourin' the country for likely lads?

2nd Shep.: Aye.

1st Shep.: When did you know it?

2nd Shep.: 'Bout a week ago.

1st Shep.: (*Reproachfully*) And ye kept a tale like that from me—and me that glad of any bit of news in this lonesomeness. I call that nasty of ye.

(2nd Shepherd *is silent; spits slowly*)

I call that nasty of ye.

2nd Shep.: Aye.

1st Shep.: And what else do ye know ye might tell me if—if, well, if I had a wee drop of something to loosen your lips—(*Pulls out a flask and a tin cup and pours a small drink—the dogs come up*) Down Jock—get out Scottie. What news have ye for this, eh?

(2nd Shepherd *reaches out his hand*)

1st Shep.: Na-na. News first. It mayn't be worth it all.

2nd Shep.: The new young lady from England is comin' this afternoon.

1st Shep.: What young lady? Why don't I know a' these wild doin's? What's she like. Who's she stayin' with?

2nd Shep.: Old man Lee and his daughter.

1st Shep.: Have you seen her? What's she like?

2nd Shep.: (*Stretching out his hand for his drink*) I've earned it.

1st Shep.: (*Drawing it away*) Ye'll tell me what she's like first.

2nd Shep.: A flower. You give it to me now.

1st Shep.: (*Hands it grudgingly*) Well, perhaps you desarve it. That's news.

(*He slowly fills a kettle out of a pail of water which he observes with annoyance is nearly empty and puts kettle on the fire*)

For why is she coming here?

2nd Shep.: London city was killin' her. The doctor ordered six months of healin' air.

1st Shep.: If she's as bonny as you say it'll be joyful doings for the young masters. Lasses are scarce here.

2nd Shep.: There's Nora Lee.

1st Shep.: Well, fule. She's only one. We've got two young masters, let alone the other young chaps hereby.

2nd Shep.: Mister Gordon's lame. What'd he do with a girl?

1st Shep.: Only a bit lame, only a wee bit lame, like—and he's got a rare brain—look at the exchange o' reapers and such like he rigged up for the freeholders around here. He's just chock full o' ideas and always dreamin' and readin' and talkin' about 'em. That's what girls like. He'll be as good in a girl's eyes as his brother—better I shouldn't wonder.

2nd Shep.: He's no good for the war.

1st Shep.: And what matters that? Am I any good for the war? Down Scottie, down will ye! Yourself is not much good for the war, and yet a pretty girl or two don't come amiss to your eyes even though they never looked at ye. War! You're crazy on the war. Why man it's more'n ten thousand miles off and it's a game for the young chaps anyway.

2ND SHEP.: It's no game.

1ST SHEP.: It'll raise the price of sheep. That's one thing I'm thinking. And we have more sheep on this station today than there have been in my memory. Aren't there now?

2ND SHEP.: Aye.

(GORDON HYDE *comes slowly on from right wing, a fishing rod and bag of fish on his shoulder. He is slight, bronzed, and with a fine noble face. He limps, his leg dragging.* 1ST SHEPHERD *takes up a tin of salmon and slowly begins to prepare to open it*)

GORDON: There's a good haul for supper, lads. (*Throws down fish*)

(THE SHEPHERDS *move a little from the fire respectfully, but don't touch their hats or get up*)

1ST SHEP.: Aye, aye, Boss.

(*He is just about to insert the tin opener,* GORDON *suddenly notices him*)

GORDON: What have you got there?

1ST SHEP.: A tin of salmon, Boss.

GORDON: Stop opening it then. Use that fresh fish instead. Tinned stuff is extra valuable nowadays. It can be sent to the front. We have time to think out here on these hills. I have thought till my head reeled and not yet found out what *big* things we can do for our country, but the little duties are clear enough, and one of 'em is not to be wasteful.

2ND SHEP.: Aye, Boss. That's true.

(1ST SHEPHERD *shamefacedly lays down the tin*)

1ST SHEP.: Eh, Boss, the sheep's fine this year.

GORDON: What is the full tally?

1ST SHEP.: Mr. Robert hasn't come in yet, but from what I've heard, it looks to be the best year on this station.

GORDON: Fine. We can't have too much wool and mutton this year.

(ROTO *comes on from left second Entrance, somewhat staggering under two pails of water. He is an old Maori, with straight black hair turning white, and a few tatoo marks on his face. He has high cheek bones, a broad nose, and full lips, but is light brown in colour and very intelligent and fine in expression. He wears a short pair of pants, and a piece of fine matting on his shoulders, his scanty shirt is open at the neck and a string with a carved green jade charm is partly seen*)

ROTO: Here is the water for Miss Nora's tea, Boss.

1st Shep.: (*To 2nd Shep.*) She has an healthier thirst than yours.

Gordon: (*Busying himself smoothing a seat of fern.*) She'll be tired after that long ride.

1st Shep.: The other lady'll be worse. She's not native born like Miss Nora.

Gordon: (*Quickly*) Her fine lady cousin! She's coming, of course. I'd forgotten! Here, you chaps, get that place straight. (*Indicates the shelter, which shows a disorder of blankets, etc.*) What is this sheep doing here?

1st Shep.: Her leg broke when she tried to push through over a rocky bit. I have tethered her down. The young lady may like to pat her or tie a ribbon round her neck perhaps.

Gordon: (*Grinning*) You old fool. All right. Leave her. Go and straighten things up a bit in the shelter. 'Tis like a pig-stye.

(*A clatter of horses hoofs, shouts of "Whoa there, Nellie. Here we are," etc., is heard without. Two Girls with riding hats and whips Enter front right wing.*

Nora Lee *is dainty with light hair and a rather sunburnt face and neck. She has pale lashes; she is petite and pretty and rather self-assured. She advances laughing*)

Nora: Here we are!

Gordon: (*Springing up and limping hurriedly to meet her, taking off his hat*) Oh, Nora, I'm glad you've come.

Nora: Where is Robert?

Gordon: Out with the men. He'll be back by tea-time.

(Loveday *stands a little back looking round and waiting. She is taller than* Nora; *a splendidly built, dark-haired and beautiful woman, with a clear skin, deep searching eyes, regular features. She walks like a Queen and has a deep-toned, but soft and thrilling voice. She is all in white*)

Nora: This is my cousin, Loveday Lewisham, Gordon.

(Loveday *smiles, comes forward and shakes hands with* Gordon)

You know I told you all about her, and how she broke down with war-work in England and is going to make her home with us for six months. *You* know.

Gordon: I do know. (*Smiles*) I wish you welcome, Miss Lewisham.

Nora: Loveday.

Gordon: Yes. This is a friendly country. My name is Gordon.

Loveday: How beautiful that view is. And *what* a ride we had. Three hours of fairyland!

NORA: Oh, that's nothing! Let us show her everything. Where's old
   Roto? She wants to see a Maori. And where is Robert?
GORDON: I'll coo-ee for Robert.
(*His coo-ee is long and penetrating so that it re-echoes*)
And there is Roto. Hi. Come along, Roto. Miss Nora wants to show
   you off.
(ROTO *advances from shelter, which is now in better order, the blankets piled
up, etc.*)
ROTO: (*Grinning*) Here, Miss Nora.
NORA: Good-day, Roto. See, Loveday. This is a real live Maori.
   Nothing wonderful after all!
LOVEDAY: Oh, how do you do?
ROTO: Finely, Miss.
LOVEDAY: (*Smiling winningly*) You are not nearly so terrifying as I
   expected!
ROTO: (*Grinning, pleased*) Maoris not allowed to be terrible now,
   Miss.
LOVEDAY: That *is* a shame. I'd so *much* rather be a savage myself.
   What do you do now they won't let you be a savage any more?
ROTO: Help with the sheep and cook.
LOVEDAY: (*Stooping forward and taking hold of* ROTO's *green jade charm
   hanging on its long string round his neck*) And what is that queer
   thing you wear round your neck?
NORA: (*Hastily*) A jade charm—these natives often wear them. They
   are very superstitious.
GORDON: The Maoris believe in all sorts of charms and magic and
   spirits. They have a legend about these forests, for instance, that a
   goddess of wisdom lives in these hill tops and is a tree by day and a
   white woman at night.
LOVEDAY: (*Her eyes sparkling*) Have you seen her?
GORDON: Not yet—but sometimes—
LOVEDAY: But sometimes—go on—do tell me—
GORDON: Sometimes after a day alone in these forests, at sunset,
   when the heavens seem opening, one half imagines Wisdom is just
   behind one, slipping between the trees—I (*hesitates*)
LOVEDAY: What an enchanting country. Tell me—
(*Sounds of arrival disturb them.* ROBERT HYDE *ENTERS. He is like*
GORDON, *but much sturdier. He is very strong and manly, with a more
sensual and less spiritual face. A very good fellow*)

NORA: Here's Robert. Robert! I have brought Loveday. This is Loveday Lewisham. She arrived last week, when you were out here. She would come so as to see a camp before you break it up. She wants to see *everything*.

(ROBERT *and* LOVEDAY *shake hands.* ROBERT *is evidently much impressed*)

ROBERT: I'll show her. (*Goes over towards fire, and points to sheep enclosures at back*) Do you see those? That's just the beginning of them. We have a rare good lot of sheep this year.

LOVEDAY: I *am* glad. We need everything good we can get this year.

ROBERT: We need everything we can get every year.

LOVEDAY: But this year specially. There are so many people in England who need extra feeding and clothing. Your sheep will be useful.

ROBERT: I hadn't thought of that.

GORDON: Wool and mutton! Both necessaries. Of course we've all thought of that, Robert.

NORA: Loveday is simply obsessed with the idea of the war, and says we ought not to have any luxuries.

2ND SHEP.: Aye. She's right.

LOVEDAY: What is that sheep doing? (*Goes toward the lame sheep by the fire*)

ROBERT: I dunno. Sick, I expect. Here, Roto. What is that sheep here for?

ROTO: Leg broke, Boss.

LOVEDAY: Oh, isn't it thirsty? Look how its tongue hangs out. Let me give it some water.

ROBERT: (*Smiling*) It doesn't want water.

LOVEDAY: Are sheep like rabbits? Don't they need water?

ROTO: (*Laughing*) Rabbits!

ROBERT: (*Smiling*) Don't you speak of rabbits to a New Zealander! Rabbits are the very devil here! We poison 'em, we shoot 'em, we trap 'em, we set dogs on 'em, we set stoats on to 'em, we imported weasels to catch 'em, we sent to Europe for ferrets to hike 'em out, we breed cats to catch 'em, we wire 'em in, and burn 'em out, and set poisoned corn over their runs, and kill 'em by thousands—but millions of 'em spring up out of the very earth and sometimes threaten to starve out the sheep, they clear the grass out. Rabbits! For the Lord's sake don't speak affectionately of rabbits.

LOVEDAY: (*Laughing mischievously*) Darling little furry things with nice white tails!

ROBERT: (*Groans*) But you're joking! Come and I'll show you why we sheep farmers hate 'em like poison.

(*THEY stroll off together. ROTO takes the empty pail and goes off. NORA and GORDON are left together*)

GORDON: (*Eagerly going, with a possessive air toward* NORA) Oh, it is wonderful to see you again!

NORA: (*Pertly, teasing him and evidently enjoying it*) Women are scarce here, I know, but there's nothing else wonderful about me.

GORDON: For me you are the dream of God which stirs the woodland, you are—(*noting her unresponsive face*) I say, do sit down. You'll be tired after that ride. Let me take your whip. Take your gloves off. Those little hands must ache after holding the reins for three hours.

NORA: Pooh! I like having the reins in my own hands.

GORDON: And so you should, they are such clever little hands.

NORA: (*Yawns affectedly*) Gordon, you're a romantic goose.

GORDON: I'm not. Everyone thinks you are wonderful, ask—

NORA: Robert doesn't think I'm at all wonderful.

GORDON: Of course he does.

NORA: Then why doesn't he tell me?

GORDON: He—he's shy. But besides, though all men may *think* such things about a girl, they only *say* them when they love her.

NORA: (*Quizzically*) So *you* love me?

GORDON: (*Tenderly*) Is it a hundred or a hundred and one times I have told you so?

NORA: And what have I answered a hundred or a hundred and one times?

GORDON: You have never once said no!

NORA: I didn't ask you what I didn't say, but what I *did* say. And what did I say?

GORDON: (*Persuasively*) Say something different this time. You can't *always* be cruel, with that sweet face you have.

NORA: Oh, can't I?

GORDON: Don't be, then.

NORA: Besides I'm not cruel. You love me. That is very nice for *you*. Being in love *is* nice. Isn't it?

GORDON: Being in love with you would make the world a heaven if only you were kind!

NORA: I am kind—to myself. Being not in love with you is much kinder to myself than what you ask. You want *me* to be happy, don't you?

GORDON: Of course! I'd die to make you happy!

NORA: I don't ask *that*. I only ask you not to talk of love.

GORDON: How can I not talk of it when I love you?

NORA: (*Turning away*) Well, if you are willing to die for me, why not stop loving me?

GORDON: No man could.

NORA: (*Flattered*) 'Um. Perhaps. But a *man* could stop talking about it. Talk of something else—anything interesting. What is Robert doing away so long?

GORDON: (*Checking his tenderness with an effort, speaking in off-hand tones*) Shewing Miss Loveday the sheep. I say, she's handsome.

NORA: Oh? *I* don't think so. But you will be soon making love to her I see. I needn't have worried about your worrying me for long.

GORDON: Don't say that, Nora. You know you are every beautiful thing to me. I hear your sweet voice every time the bell bird calls. I see your hair in the golden clouds after the sunset; I think of you and the home nest you are making somewhere, particularly when I am out here sleeping out of doors. You know I never shall think there is anyone in the world like you.

NORA: (*Peremptorily*) Stop! Where *are* Robert and Loveday? Call them, Gordon.

(GORDON *coo-ees. An answer is heard*)

GORDON: (*With a little gust of temper*) You try to prevent us being alone. You grudge me these few minutes. It is cruel.

NORA: Oh. La-la-la! (*Whistles a snatch of tune*)

(LOVEDAY *and* ROBERT *return, conversing.* LOVEDAY *comes quickly across to* NORA)

LOVEDAY: Oh, Nora, what *lots* of sheep! And the hills, how beautiful they are. The air is as clear as crystal and the sky seems so big.

GORDON: You notice that? Isn't the sky the same size in England, Miss Loveday?

LOVEDAY: No! The sky in England seems closer down on us than it is here. Our sky, even when it is blue, is as though all the smoke from all the chimneys had got on to it and weighed it down a bit.

GORDON: Everything is big here; and mostly beautiful. It makes big ideas come into one's head to be so solitary on these wide hills. Big ideas hover but they won't settle down into words, so one doesn't know clearly what they are.

LOVEDAY: (*Smiling encouragingly*) What are they about, the big ideas?

GORDON: Well, of course at present, about the war. The war is so huge one needs to be away from it, like we are here, to see how big it is.

LOVEDAY: Yes. I felt that on the voyage out, passing over those miles and miles of clean, shining blue sea. I'd worked my hardest in a tiny corner till I had broken down, in London you know, but I didn't realise what I had been working at till I was far away on the sea. Then I began to ache and ache to find some way of doing more for it than I had done. (*Whimsically*) And as I am on the sick list I seem able to do nothing at all.

GORDON: But you *have* done something. I've done nothing yet.

LOVEDAY: "Your sheep—."

GORDON: (*Smiling*) Wool and mutton are useful, I help produce those, but I must do more, Robert and I will both do more when we see clearly what we ought to do.

LOVEDAY: That's a Briton's attitude.

GORDON: I've thought of joining an Expeditionary Force, but they haven't called for us yet—and, anyway, I don't know if that *is* the best one can do—to leave all these sheep we are raising, you know. They *are* needed.

(*The beautiful note of the bell bird is heard calling through the wood*)

LOVEDAY: (*Clasping her hands*) What is that? Oh, what is that lovely note?

ROBERT
and        } (*Together*) That is the bell bird.
GORDON:

LOVEDAY: Is it wild?

NORA: Of course, it is quite common.

LOVEDAY: How clear and sweet! It is the voice of New Zealand herself, calling to her sisters all over the world, to wake, wake and sing the triumphal song of the Empire. That song will cross the waves in a thousand hearts and echo in the very centre of our lands.

NORA: Don't be a romantic goose, Loveday. The bell bird is as common as thrushes are in England.

LOVEDAY: You have so much beauty around you, has it become common to you?

ROBERT: Of course not, only we don't say much about it. You at home don't pour out poetry over every thrush that sits on a haw-hedge.

LOVEDAY: I would if I could! (*Smiling*) But I'll try not to make you think me *too* great a goose. This beautiful country has gone to my head perhaps. Everything here seems perfect!

(*Noises without of an arrival on horseback, shepherds' voices, dogs barking, etc.*

ROBERT *and* GORDON *look over their shoulders and exchange a knowing grin*)

ROBERT: I think I hear the voice of *one* in perfection!

(*ENTER* JOHN VARLIE. *He is a florid man, with rather bulging eyes, a clean shaven face, with a noticeable but small triangular scar on the right cheek, one eyelid slightly more closed than the other. He wears American clothes and speaks with a strong American accent. He is accompanied by the shepherds and dogs*)

VARLIE: Waal, boys! Here we are again. I have just delivered your new shearing gear down at your homestead and they told me down in the valley I should strike your trail up here, so I flicked up my grey mare to keep you from feelin' lonesome without me.

ROBERT: (*Amiably*) Halloo, Varlie. We aren't lonesome today.

VARLIE: (*Looking from one to the other*) The ladies! I just can't quit now though I guess I'm as little wanted as a bug in a blanket.

ROBERT: Not a wet blanket anyway.

GORDON: You're welcome. We'll show you off. Miss Loveday Lewisham is fresh out from home and wants to see all the native sights. Miss Loveday, this is Mr. John Varlie, the universal provider. A regular conjurer who wafts the appliances of civilisation into our rude wilderness.

VARLIE: Miss Lewisham, I'm proud to make your acquaintance. Say, cut that Hyde. I'm no conjurer. I'm a plain business man, and only doing what any other business man could do if he had the brains.

ROBERT: That's it. It takes a Yankee to think of selling the goods we want in this part of the British Empire.

LOVEDAY: What do you want?

VARLIE: (*Slapping his leg*) What I've got here, Miss Lewisham.

NORA: (*A little spitefully*) I often thought you used your brains to make them think they wanted to buy what you wanted to sell.

VARLIE: Aw—come now, Miss Nora. You're real cute, but you don't think I could monkey with British brains?

NORA: (*Lightly*) Well, the British brains in *my* neighbourhood are not fair game for you. (*Looks at* ROBERT) They don't know what they ought to want (*looks at* GORDON) or they want what they can't get.

VARLIE: Well, they all ought to have *this*! (*Produces sample tin opener from his pocket. The* SHEPHERDS *look eagerly on*) Is there a tin of food stuff around? Surely?

ROTO: Here you are, Boss.

(*Runs to the shelter and returns with one*)

VARLIE: Now this tin opener won't only save your breath, but it'll let the recording angel have a holiday. See that? (*Has slit the tin round rapidly and easily*) Can you beat that with any tin opener you ever set eyes on?

1ST SHEP.: Noa. That'll be a useful kind—if they all work as easy.

2ND SHEP.: Aye.

GORDON: Bully for you.

VARLIE: How many will you take? You chaps ought to have one each. And the ladies! There will be a day when the ladies are alone to get the supper, none of you handy Herculeses around. With this opener, getting the supper is as easy as smiling. Now then! Only sixpence each. Finest American non-rusting steel.

NORA: Fancy wasting your time with such a trifle, Mr. Varlie.

VARLIE: Don't fret. I ain't wastin' my time. I came around your homestead with the big dump of machinery. And I am like the elephant's trunk, calculated to pull up a tree or pick up a pin. (*Laughter*) I'm picking up more than you think, maybe.

LOVEDAY: (*Smiling and counting the people*) One, two, three, why there are six of us, if we have one each all round! You don't mean to tell me that you have six tin openers in your pocket?

VARLIE: Yep. 'N I've got a pack horse over there with sixty on it, and sixty dozen in Dunedin, and sixty thousand where they came from! Now, you'll have one, Miss?

LOVEDAY: Yes, I will.

VARLIE: Bully. And you—

(GORDON *takes it half laughing*)

GORDON: All right.

VARLIE: And you—

ROBERT: Not I My jack knife has a claw that's good enough for me.

VARLIE: Now, Mr. Hyde, just let me. . .

(*Leads* ROBERT *aside and tries to persuade him. Meanwhile there is a clatter without as of several horses arriving. A* RECRUITING OFFICER *and two or three* YOUNG MEN, *all in khaki* ENTER *as if just from horseback after a long ride.*

VARLIE *steps aside whispering with* 1ST SHEPHERD)

RE: OFF. Hey, lads. They told me I should find a covey of you here. Fine! I'm glad we struck your camp. Whew! We're dead thirsty! Have you got any tea?

GORDON: Sure. Those kettles are boiling. We'll have tea in a jiffy.

ROBERT: Where are you going?

RE. OFF: Zig-zagging cross country to the outlying stations.

(VARLIE *aside, whispering with* 1ST SHEPHERD. *The word "Germany" is overheard*)

1ST SHEP.: (*Indignantly*) Are you askin' who around here sympathises with Germany?

VARLIE: (*Annoyed*) No, no, you fool! You ain't got me square! (*Shuts up note-book with a snap and turns away*)

1ST SHEP.: Are you square?

VARLIE: (*Tipping him*) Here's to prove it. (*The* SHEPHERD *takes the money, but looks rather distrustfully at* VARLIE. *They separate*)

NORA: (*To* RECRUITING OFFICER) My! But you look fine! That's the first khaki we've seen round here.

RE. OFF: It'll not be the last, Miss. Khaki breeds khaki.

ROTO: (*Chuckles. Suddenly, to* ROBERT) He is the colour of a rabbit, Boss, that's why.

ROBERT: Shut up, you fool. This is serious.

LOVEDAY: (*Laughs*) Rabbits? (*She looks mischievously at* ROBERT)

GORDON: Sit down and have tea first, and then tell us all about it.

RE. OFF: Thanks. (*To his* MEN) You may sit down too, lads. We've ridden hard. But first water the horses.

(*One of his* MEN *goes out with pails, assisted by* ROTO. *Splashing and champing sounds are heard. In a few minutes* THEY *return and sit with the rest*)

ROBERT: Are you recruiting?

RE. OFF: You've hit it, my lad. (*Takes off his hat and wipes his forehead*)

NORA: Let's see your hat. It is smart.

RE. OFF: (*Flattered, passes it*) There, miss.

(NORA *leans over to* LOVEDAY *and they examine it together.* NORA *takes off her own and coquettishly tries it on, catches* ROBERT's *eye, he smiles and looks away; catches* GORDON's *eye, he gazes admiringly at her, she tosses her head and takes the hat off. Mugs of tea are handed round, the men drink thirstily*)

VARLIE: (*Remaining, eagerly listening, leans over to* RECRUITING OFFICER) Say, stranger, are you getting along well with your job?

RE. OFF: (*Keenly*) And who are you?

VARLIE: Waal, I guess it can't be hard for you to lay your finger on the name of my country.

RE. OFF: I asked you.

VARLIE: I'm an Amurrican.

RE. OFF: Passports all right?

VARLIE: (*Affecting laziness, drawing them out*) I should say.

(RECRUITING OFFICER *examines them, looks at him keenly, and passes them back*)

ROBERT: *He's* all right, Officer! We have had him around the station many a time.

NORA: He's the only man with brains enough to sell us the things we want.

ROBERT: He has brains enough to sell us the things we *don't* want.

RE. OFF: Brains are always suspicious.

ROBERT: Oh, I say! That's being *too* British! *He's* all right. *Some* straight men have brains.

GORDON: And lots of straight men are muddled headed enough to think that wasting peoples time making a lot of truck nobody wants is good for trade.

RE. OFF: Pardon. This tea's good. Have you more, Missy?

NORA: As much as *you* want—Officer! Is that what I should call you?

RE. OFF: That'll do for me fine, Missy.

NORA: Fill up the kettle, Roto.

RE. OFF: Now my men. 'tenshun. (*All three rise*) We'll have our meeting.

(ROTO *returns, and he and the* SHEPHERDS *crowd eagerly behind the others listening*)

LOVEDAY: But we seem like friends now, are you going to give us a formal speech?

RE. OFF: When we speak of our King and Country we stand up to it like men, Miss.

LOVEDAY: Then *so* do we.

(*She springs up. All rise and stand round the* RECRUITING OFFICER *who is flanked by his own men*)

RE: OFF. God Save the King.

ALL: God Save the King.

(*A fleeting sneer is seen on* VARLIE'S *face, but he shouts louder than any*)

RE: OFF. (*Oratorically*) We have lived in New Zealand, some for years, some of us all our lives, and we know what New Zealand means to us. And most of us also know the Old Dart, know her and love her.

SEVERAL: Hear, hear!

LOVEDAY: (*Whispering*) The Old Dart, what's that?

ROBERT: (*Smiling down on her*) That's England, Great Britain, our pet name for the Old Country.

RE. OFF: Now the Old Dart's in trouble, fighting for her life—and, my lads, it's not only her life, it's *our* life, too, she's fighting for. Like a mother fightin' for her young. And, she's not only fightin for her young, which is us, she is fightin' for the world! for decency, and truth, for liberty.

ALL: (*Increasingly enthusiastic*) Hear, hear! That's right. Bravo.

RE. OFF: She's fightin' for liberty, fightin' so that promises shall be kept between nations as decent men keep 'em between each other.

(*A murmur of assent*)

> You know if your neighbours were all the time to lie to you over everything they promised to do, you would never be able to keep going with them. Like a man, you'd have to up and show 'em what's what. And that's what the Old Dart is doing, and it is a big fight. But it is going on in Europe, which is more than 10,000 miles away from us. You may ask what has it all to do with *us*?

ROBERT
and
GORDON: } Not us. We know. We *don't* ask what it has to do with us!

RE. OFF: (*Hesitates as if thrown off his track*) Then you don't need my speech. (*Suddenly brightens and smiles appealingly*) Don't spoil my speech lads. Pretend to ask so you can hear it. It will make you feel real grand.

ROBERT
and
GORDON: } Fire away then. Hear, hear!

ROTO: (*Excited*) That's it, Mister. Give it us.

RE. OFF: (*Continues more eloquently*) Now we are New Zealanders, and we live in this free and happy land, you may ask, what has all this trouble in Europe to do with us?

ROBERT,
GORDON
*and the* } Hear! Hear! We do, we do ask!
SHEPHERDS

RE. OFF: (*Very effectively*) But I answer you lads, what language do we speak? English! What race are we? Britons! Why, lads, the British over there aren't as British as we are; They are English and Scotch and Irish and Welsh—but what are we? All these British strains mixed! Most of us have some Scotch blood and some English blood and some Irish blood mixed in our veins, many of us have been to other parts of Britain and got a touch of Canada, or Australia, or South Africa into us. I say lads we are *more* British than the folks in the Old Dart. We are a fine blend of all the flavours of different Britons, we are the very essence of Britain! We are epitomes of Empire.

ALL: (*Enthusiastic*) Hurray, that's right. Hear, hear! Go it!

ROTO: (*Particularly enthusiastic*) We are, we are, hear, hear, Boss!

1ST SHEP.: (*Digging* ROTO *in the ribs*) Ho, Ho!

RE. OFF: Do I need to tell you it's a righteous war?

GORDON: We know that!

ROBERT: Shut up, let him give us his speech!

RE. OFF: (*Smiling*) I wasn't going into that. I don't have to tell our lads it's a righteous war. I only asked it like a rhetorical question this time.

ROTO: Go on, Boss, go on. You speak most as fine as a Maori chief.

RE. OFF: Now, if Britons are engaged in this war, *we* are engaged, for are we not the Britons of the British? We are. And lads, I will tell you, in the words of our own Prime Minister, Mr. Massey himself, I say to you that *"All that we have and are is staked upon the issue of the war!"*

ALL: (*Tremendous enthusiasm*) Hear, hear, bravo, hurrah!

(*A roar of sound drowns the actual words.* VARLIE *shouts, but has a slight sneering smile on his lips as he watches the generous enthusiasm of the others*)

RE. OFF: Now lads, you know we are free Britons in this country. We expect every New Zealander will do his duty because he's glad, aye and proud to do it. You are all only waiting to be told what to do.

We have no compulsion. But when you know what we are going to do, you'll all want to join in.

SHEPHERDS: Tell us Mister.

RE. OFF: We are a small nation. Only about a million souls of us altogether, counting women and children. Now that's very small as nations go. But what are we going to do? We are going to put a larger number of troops in the field than the British had in the great battle of Waterloo!

(ALL *at first incredulous, then wildly enthusiastic*)

RE. OFF: Aye, Aye, lads. Well may you shout. That's what comes of being New Zealand Britons. But we are going to do more. We are going to do what the experts tell us is the most possible that any nation *can* do; in three years we are going to have ten per cent. of our total population in the field! That's the maximum, the absolute scientific limit of what any nation *can* put in. And that means from our little country we shall send one hundred thousand men to the field.

ALL: Hurray, hurray!

LOVEDAY: (*Glowing*) How splendid, how splendid you are!

RE. OFF: That's it Missy, that's how New Zealand women take it.

ROBERT: She's English, she's just visiting from home!

RE. OFF: From the Old Dart? Our men'll follow you back Missy, all of us would like to, only the years have passed over some, and that ties 'em. When the years press on your shoulders you can't carry the knapsack too! And I see some of you chaps are too old.

1ST SHEP.: (*Groans*) I am, curse the day I was born.

RE. OFF: But all of you, every one of you has your part to play. If you can't fight you can *save*. That's what the people of New Zealand haven't realised yet. How many of our patriots have reduced their consumption of petrol or of beer by a single gallon because of their patriotism? Yet that is what they must do. That's what we all must do.

*Men must fight*
*And women must save*
*The path of glory for Britons to pave.*

(LOVEDAY *and* GORDON *stand a little apart and are talking*)

GORDON: Ah, this stirs one! I wonder if *this* is what I ought to do?

LOVEDAY: (*Smilingly shakes her head*) I don't know.

GORDON: A man has only one life. That's all he *can* give to his country.

LOVEDAY: But the thousands of sheep you raise may be even more useful! (*mischievously*) It is a question you know—is one man as much use to his country as his ten thousand sheep?

GORDON: Old men can raise sheep.

RE. OFF: (*Louder, catching all eyes*) And now to come to the fighting element. I've just said, all of you can do *something*. But those of you who can fight are wanted now. Have you seen this paper? (*Takes official set of questions out of his pocket*)

MEN: (*Shaking their heads*) No. What is it?

RE. OFF: Then I'll read it to you. It is addressed to all men between nineteen and forty-five. Which of you are between nineteen and forty-five?

GORDON: (*Looks across at* LOVEDAY *and says to her alone*) That's a direct message to me.

(GORDON, ROBERT, ROTO *and the* 2ND SHEPHERD *stand out, each saying* "*I am!*")

RE. OFF: (*Slapping* ROTO *on the shoulder*) How old are you?

ROTO: (*Quickly*) Forty-five, Mister.

RE. OFF: Open your mouth.

(ROTO *opens and shows browned teeth*)

RE. OFF: (*Laughing*) Forty-five, with that hair and those teeth!

ROTO: (*Protesting*) I am, I am. My hair gone pale when I was nearly drowned in the Rotorua hot spring.

RE. OFF: Get out.

ROTO: (*Persistently*) I'm strong man. I'm young man, see my muscle. Feel my arm.

RE. OFF: You are not a Pakeha. You can't fight with the Pakeha.

LOVEDAY: (*To* NORA) What is Pakeha? What does he mean?

NORA: Pakeha are white men, Englishmen.

ROTO: (*Protesting*) My father was a Queen-Maori.

RE. OFF: Was he? That's good.

LOVEDAY: Whatever is a Queen-Maori?

RE. OFF: In the great war, missy, the Maori war, the Maoris who fought on the side of the English, under Queen Victoria, you know, they were called Queen-Maoris.

ROTO: My father fought with Pakeha then, why not me today? Take me. I am strong like the branches of the Kauri pine. I am hard as my hei-tiki. My father was a Queen-Maori. I will be a Queen-Maori and fight for you. Take me.

RE. OFF: You are too old. You are sixty years old if you are a minute.

ROTO: No, no.

RE. OFF: (*To the* 1ST SHEPHERD) He is on your station, isn't he? How old is he?

1ST SHEP.: Well, we don't know exactly. But it is about six years ago since we had a feast and a good drink because he said it was his fiftieth birthday.

RE. OFF: There! Stand aside my man. If you are so strong you must do the work the young men leave behind them.

(ROTO *protests, and expresses chagrin but says no more*)

RE. OFF: (*To* GORDON *not noticing his lameness as he stands with the others*) How old are you, sir?

GORDON: Twenty-nine.

RE. OFF: (*To* ROBERT) And you, sir?

ROBERT: Thirty-one.

RE. OFF: Good! (*To* 2ND SHEPHERD) And you?

2ND SHEP.: Forty-two.

RE. OFF: H'm. You look more.

2ND SHEP.: I'm forty-two (*glares*)

RE. OFF: (*Feeling his arm and looking at him*) H'm. Well. Now lads. On this paper are the following questions addressed specially to you as you are between nineteen and forty-five. Question A. Have you volunteered for military service beyond New Zealand as a member of an Expeditionary Force in connection with the present war? If so, have you been accepted for service or rejected?

ALL THREE: No. No, Boss. No.

RE. OFF: Well, Question B. If you have *not* volunteered for service, are you, being a single man without dependants, willing to become a member of an Expeditionary Force? or (2) Are you—? By the way, let's settle that first. Are you all single men?

ALL THREE: Yes. Yes. Yes, sir.

RE. OFF: Then I needn't read the alternative questions. Are you willing to become members of an Expeditionary Force?

ALL THREE: Yes.

RE. OFF: That's right, lads. Now I'll be honest with you, and tell you that all the law asks of you is to sign copies of this paper and send them in—you will get them officially in a few days maybe—but that's not what *I'm* here for, to get from you a mere scrap of paper with a promise for the future on it. I'm here to get you yourselves, lads, now. That's better fitted to a Briton than to write his name on a bit of paper, and to go back to his ordinary job! He that puts his hand to the plough and turns back—you know what it says in the Bible. You lads, and I, have got acquainted this afternoon, and I know you're not *that* kind.

ALL THREE: No! We are not! We'll come now, right now!

ROBERT: (*Taking a step forward*) I'll come at once. That's square. (*Looking at* LOVEDAY *and smiling*) Can you fit me out in khaki right now, Officer?

RE. OFF: The doctor'll have to examine you (*indicating one of the men with him*) and you'll have to take the oath.

ROBERT: Yes, yes. Surely you have an extra uniform handy!

RE. OFF: (*Smiling*) It's very irregular, sir. We'll see later, step aside.

GORDON: Now me.

RE. OFF: (*Examines him more carefully. Speaking kindly*) Step across to me, sir.

(GORDON *tries to conceal his limp as much as possible, but of course fails*)

RE. OFF: (*Shaking his head*) No good, sir. Why, you're lame!

GORDON: Hardly at all. And I'm strong! I've never been ill. I can ride day and night in the saddle. I'd join the mounted rifles!

RE. OFF: Not a bit of good, sir.

GORDON: (*Unbelieving*) I'm the right age. I'm strong. I can ride like a cow-boy. I can shoot better than my brother.

ROBERT: That's so.

RE. OFF: Your bit is not at the front.

LOVEDAY: Oh, officer. Is it impossible? It is such a *trifling* limp.

(GORDON *looks acutely distressed but smiles bravely and very gratefully at* LOVEDAY)

RE. OFF: Not a bit more good than if *you* was to ask, Missy.

GORDON: (*Half stammering in his eagerness*) You must take me, *somehow* or other. You must. I can shoot. I never miss my aim! What is the good of coming here and rousing us all up with your talk of soldiering if you won't take the best shot in the place?

RE. OFF: (*Kindly*) You'll do no fighting, sir.

GORDON: (*Overcome*) Curse the tree that staked me! Curse the fools that didn't heal me square!

(*There is an awkward silence. He flings up to* Nora, *who is a little apart from the rest, his eyes blazing*)

Gordon: Nora, what do you say? Aren't I fit to go?

Nora: (*Calmly*) Of course not, Gordon. I can't think how you could have expected—

Gordon: (*Wildly*) Now I see why you never loved me! You've teased me often enough. I've made love like a man, but to you, to *you* I was never a man! I see it now. You all think me useless. You don't look on me as a *man*!

(*A tense pause,* Loveday *and* Robert *look rather awkwardly distressed*)

Nora: (*Somewhat cowed*) Don't be silly.

Robert: I say, old chap, don't take it so hard.

Gordon: Wouldn't you take it hard if both your country and the woman you love told you plainly you were mere useless rubbish?

Loveday: (*Pitifully*) Perhaps you will find a still greater thing to do for your country. It is not *only* fighters she needs.

Gordon: (*His lips quivering*) You are kind. But, oh God!—

(*He goes toward shelter away from the* Others *and aimlessly unfolds the blankets, folds them up again, and re-arranges the pile; opens them out and re-folds them, and so on.*

*Meanwhile, the* Recruiting Officer *has quietly asked questions of the* 2nd Shepherd, *whose answers are satisfactory.*

Loveday *looks from one to the other, then sits brooding, glancing pitifully at* Gordon *from time to time.*

*While this is going on, the* Recruiting Officer *takes* Robert *and the* 2nd Shepherd *out, followed by the men with him, leaving* Nora, 1st Shepherd, Roto *and* Varlie *in a group.* Loveday *a little apart*)

Roto: (*Grumbling, to* 1st Shepherd) You have a black heart, you Pakeha tutua.

1st Shep.: Trying to lie about your age? You are older than I am.

Roto: Why not lie about your age, too?

1st Shep.: What would become of the sheep if I went off? Are the sheep to die on the hills because the Germans are scurvy dogs? And the best lot of sheep we have had, too, since I've been on the station!

Nora: When will you black fellows learn not to tell lies? What is the good of telling lies any way, when you are always found out?

Roto: I wouldn't have been if he hadn't wagged his tongue! And to tell a bit of a lie so to give your life, that's no lie.

　　　　　　　　　　　　　　　　　　　　　　　　MARIE STOPES

VARLIE: Ah, Miss Nora, don't try to stamp out necessary lying. The world would be in a queer way if none of us told lies once in a way. I'll wager you this patent button hook you tell lies yourself now and then. Little ones!

NORA: (*Smiling*) Oh, well—when I say I'm glad to see you, for instance, that's not a lie. It doesn't take you in!

VARLIE: Freeze on to the button hook, Miss Nora. I've won my wager. It is only sixpence.

NORA: (*Tosses it back to him*) What are you dreaming about, Loveday?

LOVEDAY: Before ever I met you all—for months past—I have been thinking about Gordon's problem. What is one who cannot fight to do for our country?

NORA: Save, as you said yourself.

LOVEDAY: It isn't only fighting and saving the nation's needs. It needs *thinking*. Wouldn't it be splendid to see a man's strength and his brains put into thinking that might save thousands of lives in the time to come.

VARLIE: People who talk about thinking are generally fools. The wise man thinks his hardest how to conceal what he is thinking.

LOVEDAY: (*Swiftly and scornfully*) That's a worldly man, whose thoughts are grasping. I was dreaming of a man whose thoughts would be *gifts*.

VARLIE: Thoughts are pretty cheap gifts.

LOVEDAY: Is there anything we possess that did not grow from a thought? Isn't the freedom in your country the result of the thought of the men who framed your Constitution? Isn't all law, all order, all happiness, thought, or the results of it?

VARLIE: Huh! That's too deep for me.

NORA: (*Reproving*) You are such a dreamer, Loveday. It's so woolly to dream, stop it.

LOVEDAY: My dreams are beginning to clear. If no one had ever thought, we would be savages still. All human beings would be tearing out each other's eyes, always.

VARLIE: Yep. But talking about *my* thoughts is not my job. (*Yawning*) I must be getting along. When are those fellows going to start?

(*Sounds of cheering and laughter and trampling without.* ROBERT *comes swaggering on in a Khaki uniform with hat jauntily tilted. He is followed by the* 2ND SHEPHERD *with Badge and Armlet.* RECRUITING OFFICER *and his* MEN *follow, grinning. The group round the fire start up. All crowd round* ROBERT *shouting, admiring and patting him on the back.* ROBERT *goes up to* LOVEDAY *and salutes her, she smiles at him cheerily*)

LOVEDAY: Bravo! How fine you look!

(*She looks past him however, to where* GORDON *is wistfully watching the group, and mastering himself to come forward. She smiles very sweetly and encouragingly at* GORDON. *The sky slowly takes on sunset tints*)

NORA: (*To* ROBERT) Give me one of your buttons. I'll wear it.

ROBERT: (*Putting her off, with forced gaiety*) With the officer looking? Shame on you!

NORA: (*To* RECRUITING OFFICER) A man who's enlisted is allowed to give away *one* button, isn't he?

RE. OFF: (*Smiling*) One—only one—to the girl he loves.

NORA: (*Invitingly*) Now, Robert, you hear!

(GORDON *overhears this and waits eagerly for* ROBERT'S *answer*)

ROBERT: (*Laughs and comically struts*) Don't shear my feathers off me yet!

NORA: (*To* VARLIE) Men *are* vain.

VARLIE: Take one of *my* buttons! (*Holds out his coat*)

NORA: (*Eyes flashing*) When you're in khaki!

GORDON: (*Pulling himself together, holds out his hand to* ROBERT, *speaks huskily*) Good luck, old chap, the best of luck!

(LOVEDAY *looks proudly at* GORDON)

ROBERT: (*Claps* GORDON'S *shoulder with his free hand*) Keep the station going till I come back, sonny.

GORDON: I will, Robert.

ROBERT: *If* I come back!

NORA: (*Excitedly*) Of course you will. You'll come back with a V.C., won't he, lads?

ALL: Of course. He's just the make of a hero. Hurrah! Bravo!

(ALL *crowd round him shouting and singing snatches of "Rule Britannia, God Save the King," etc.*

The sunset is crimson by now)

ROBERT: Look at the sky! Come, we must be getting back.

(ALL *follow him, marching, waving branches, etc., singing, "See the Conquering hero comes." The rest troop off, but* ROBERT *turns and goes up to* LOVEDAY *who is lingering and keeps her apart*)

ROBERT: Wait a minute, won't you?

LOVEDAY: Yes? Of course, what is it?

ROBERT: (*Shyly*) I say, I—won't you—(*he takes out his jack knife and cuts off a button, offering it to her*) I say, won't you, won't you wear it, just to bring me luck?

LOVEDAY: (*Hesitates*) Oh—I—

ROBERT: Of course I don't mean—to—to bother you in any way. I mean it only in—in friendship! Just to bring me luck. Do! There's nothing in it—nothing silly—like what *they* said.

LOVEDAY: (*Smiling, very charmingly*) Shall I sew it on again for you?

ROBERT: Oh! If you *won't* have it—you may sew it on if I may keep my coat on while you are doing it!

LOVEDAY: Very well. Heroes have to be humoured, I suppose. Come along, it's getting late!

(*THEY follow the others, as she is going off she looks back and sends a compassionate glance towards* GORDON.

*The sky rapidly darkens.* GORDON *stays behind, waits till they are all out of sight, then he throws himself face down on the ground, clenching his hands and moving as though in pain. The bell bird's clear sweet note is heard. He lies in silence then groans aloud*)

GORDON: To both my country and the woman I love, I'm not a man. I'm lumber—useless lumber! Nora! Nora!

(GORDON *crouches in despair. The stage is now dusky, a pale moon shows. Softly, without any noise, between the trunks of two tall trees appears behind him the upper part of a white figure, with the forehead and head half covered by a floating white veil; the face is tender and grave, the eyes glowing as if inspired. In the shadowy light the figure looks like a vision.* GORDON *does not recognise that it is* LOVEDAY. *He slowly, as if mesmerised, rises on to his knees. There is a sweet low call of the bell bird far away. Stillness for a moment.* LOVEDAY *stands silent between the trees*)

GORDON: (*Still half kneeling, speaking in awed tones*) You are a spirit?

(LOVEDAY *is quite still*)

GORDON: You are the goddess of the woods come to me in my pain! Tell me, you beautiful, you wonderful—tell me, what have I to do? Speak to me, speak to me!

(LOVEDAY *does not move; in a soft, penetrating voice, she intones, like a chant*)

LOVEDAY: The bodies of men that can fight are mown down like the grass.

The body of one young man, even if he is a prince among men cannot slay more than a hundred of his enemies.

But by thought a man's brain might conceive of a way to kill or to save hundreds of thousands.

Now is the time for a Briton to arise who can slay with his great thought all the enemies of the future.

Now is the time for one to bring forth a noble plan, so that all the treacherous aggressors shall be for ever disarmed and the peaceful nations be for ever free from fear of onslaught.

(*She draws the veil across her face, takes a step back into the dusk and vanishes*)

GORDON: (*Exalted and trembling with eagerness*) Angel! Goddess! Tell me—how—

(*She does not return and makes no sound*)

*Slowly the CURTAIN descends.*

# Act II

*Three or Four months later than Act I.*

*The Hyde's Homestead, S. Island, New Zealand. Left back, one end of the low homestead with its broad, creeper-covered verandah abuts on to the garden. A rough piece of road runs across right back of stage. Back cloth painted with luxurious vegetation and vivid blue sky. Mixture of common English fruit trees and Eucalyptus, the lily-palm, masses of crimson ratas in flower.*

GORDON HYDE *and* LOVEDAY DISCOVERED *sitting together in garden, down right.* GORDON *has a sheaf of papers and writing pad on his knee, pen in hand.* LOVEDAY *is chewing the end of a flower stalk as though thinking.*

GORDON: (*Laying down papers and looking at* LOVEDAY *with friendship and admiration in his eyes, but not love*) It *is* good of you coming over so often to help me. I don't know what I should have done without you. The others try to slay with laughter all my young ideas. I *am* indebted to you!

LOVEDAY: No, no! It has been simply splendid for me to see you work out these great ideas. It has been wonderful to watch the little germ of your conception grow and grow and take practical shape in your wonderful brain!

GORDON: Oh, it is not mine. None of all this (*indicating papers on his knee*) is mine. All my ideas before that day had been vague and muddled. Now I am only writing down the ideas that vision, that goddess gave me.

LOVEDAY: The practical ideas *are* yours.

GORDON: No.

LOVEDAY: Yes. Indeed they are, I've watched you shaping them.

GORDON: No. The germ of everything was in that beautiful message she gave me.

LOVEDAY: (*Looking at him as though acquiescing tenderly to humour him. He does not see the look*) Who was it do you think?

GORDON: A spirit.

LOVEDAY: (*Triumphantly*) There *are* no spirits you know—no spirits that talk to living people. The ideas are your own, your very own—

GORDON: Perhaps the Maoris are right. This *was* a spirit. It *couldn't* have been imagination! I heard her speak quite clearly. Her wonderful voice was like music, thrilling and deep like the songs of birds in a cool, deep glade.

LOVEDAY: But you were overwrought. Imagination plays tricks then.

GORDON: Yes, I was overwrought. That recruiting business had amazingly stirred me. But what she said was so remote from my misery that I *could* not have imagined anything so vital, so full of hope. I felt shamed, anguished. I felt my manhood beaten in the dust, by my country, by the woman I loved.

LOVEDAY: (*Murmurs*) No, no.

GORDON: Do you know what love is? Have you ever loved? If not, you could never understand my shame.

LOVEDAY: I have never loved—

(*His face is averted, she looks at him long and tenderly*)

    until—

GORDON: Ah, but you—beautiful and radiant as you are will never know what it is to have love *spurned*—as I have.

LOVEDAY: I'm not—so—sure!

GORDON: (*Eagerly*) Are you not sure that my love is spurned? Do you think Nora, after all, may love me?

LOVEDAY: That's—that's not quite what I meant. But—when—when once Nora sees how the great world honours you for these ideas (*taps papers on his knee*) she will love you, she must. All women will love you and bless you—for you will be the saviour of their sons!

GORDON: But Nora is so living—so—*feminine*. I don't think dreamy things like *ideas* appeal to her. Oh, how well I remember her as a girl with her golden hair flying! We three were brought up together, she and Robert and I She never cared about reading, but always played some real game.

LOVEDAY: As she gets older she will see that ideas are real. Perhaps, and then—

GORDON: Wish that for me!

LOVEDAY: Are you sure you wish it for yourself?

GORDON: Sure! Wish it for me! There is something wonderful about you. Your wishes would bring me luck.

LOVEDAY: I wish you every, every happiness.

GORDON: That's vague. Say, "I wish that Nora may love you and make you happy."

LOVEDAY: I wish that if Nora loves you she may make you happy.

GORDON: Ah, *if* (*suddenly looking at her*) What's the matter with you? Your voice sounds tired. Are you tired?

LOVEDAY: Yes. That's it. I am a little tired.

GORDON: We'll stop the work.

LOVEDAY: No, no. See. I'll come here in the shade. (*She moves where he can't see her face*) Now read over some of what you have written, and I'll listen critically.

GORDON: (*Looks at her for a moment, then reads*) "The nations shall unite and have a super-parliament to which they shall all send a small number of representatives. This super-parliament shall make International laws, but it shall chiefly exist to prevent any nation flying at another's throat. If necessary, by force." (*In another tone*) Flying at another's throat, doesn't seem formal enough, does it?

LOVEDAY: Perhaps not. Mark it. Go on.

GORDON: "In order to prevent any murderously-minded nation flying at another's throat (*in different tone*) as Germany did at Belgium. *That* example will never be forgotten."

LOVEDAY: Never. But go on.

GORDON: "In order to prevent for ever," I'll add for ever, shall I?

LOVEDAY: Yes.

GORDON: "In order for ever to prevent any murderously-minded nation flying at another's throat, or stealing any of the rights, or breaking any international law, the super-parliament shall have behind it the whole of the armaments of the world." That's good, isn't it? *That's* the point.

LOVEDAY: Splendid! That's where your scheme differs from all the dear crack-brained pacificists. Have you written out the clauses by which that is secured?

GORDON: Yes. (*Shuffles the papers*) "The super-parliament is to have complete control of all the armies and all the armament factories in the whole world. Any individual or group of individuals violating that monopoly and attempting private manufacture of armaments shall be subject to instant death."

LOVEDAY: Good!

GORDON: You are bloodthirsty!

LOVEDAY: I am only cruel to villains to be kind to the virtuous. But I'm afraid a really sneak-dog nation, like—well, like *some* we could mention, would have made armaments secretly and piled them up.

GORDON: No, no, because—(*shuffles the papers*) Where is it? There is to be a clause preventing any such hanky-panky.

LOVEDAY: There is no doubt, that if that is managed properly, however greedy or treacherous any individual nation might be, it simply wouldn't *dare* to go to war.

GORDON: That's the idea.

LOVEDAY: And that is a much more practical idea than that of the pacificists who talk about *voluntary* limitation of armaments.

GORDON: They idealise human nature.

LOVEDAY: Now *your* plan *compels* decent behaviour.

GORDON: *Don't* call it mine. It is all the gift of my fairy genius of the woods.

LOVEDAY: (*Smiling as though tenderly humouring him*) Have you seen her again—your spirit in the woods?

GORDON: No, only that once.

LOVEDAY: Well, what you told me of her words then was just the vague dream of an idea, but look at all these sheets and sheets of carefully worked out clauses. All these actual, practical, useful ideas are *yours*!

GORDON: They are not. Though I was dreaming and longing vaguely for something of the kind, I'm not big enough actually to have thought it out.

LOVEDAY: You are. You are big enough for anything!

GORDON: Nora doesn't think so.

LOVEDAY: (*Scornfully*) Nora!

GORDON: Why are you so keen on making me think too well of myself?

LOVEDAY: Not too well.

GORDON: Why do you trouble that I should even think well of myself at all?

LOVEDAY: Because when a man is a man he should respect himself as one man respects another.

GORDON: You are wonderful—women generally try to make a man feel a worm.

LOVEDAY: (*Hastily*) What I like best about this splendid scheme of *yours* is, that even Germany will *have* to accept it when it is proposed to her, because she is all the while demanding "only her own national safety," and pretending she has no aggressive desires, so she can't have the face to refuse to join in—and yet when she does her militarism will be choked. Nothing could destroy all militarism more completely than this!

GORDON: Yes. And she would give herself away so utterly if she stood out!

LOVEDAY: And if she *did* stand out, she'd—

(NORA, *with a basket of fruit on her arm, enters from road*)

NORA: (*Laughing*) Halloo, you two? At it again? Settling the affairs of the world in *this* remote spot!

GORDON: Why not? Every spot is remote from somewhere else.

NORA: London is not remote from the war, and *if* your ideas aren't boiled gooseberries, they had better get to London.

LOVEDAY: Of course they will get to London. All ideas reach London in the end.

GORDON: Robert left me here on trust. I must keep his sheep going, at any rate till I can get a responsible manager. Then I'll go to London.

NORA: London has got too many ideas of its own to listen to an utterly unknown New Zealand sheep farmer.

GORDON: (*Sighing*) It may take time!

NORA: (*Laughing*) Time! It'll take more than time. You don't know a soul in London.

GORDON: I don't, that's flat.

LOVEDAY: *I* do.

NORA: *You* do? Of course you do. You will have to write him introductions. How will you begin? "A young genius, called Gordon Hyde, has ideas to set the Thames on fire. For love of me please give him a match"—or—"Gordon Hyde is my dear friend, and a dear fool, and as sometimes fools rush in where angels fear to tread, please send him in your motor car at once to the Prime Minister."

(*Both laugh, though* GORDON *flushes as if somewhat hurt*)

LOVEDAY: You laugh because you don't know how powerful a really great idea is.

NORA: I don't. Perhaps because I've never met one.

LOVEDAY: (*Seeing* GORDON *looking wistfully at* NORA, *rises*) Here, Gordon, give me those papers. We have done enough for the present. I'll take them into the house. (*She saunters along the verandah and enters the house*)

GORDON: Sit down, Nora. You'll be tired after picking all that fruit. I'll carry it over for you when you are rested.

NORA: I can carry it quite well myself. I'm every bit as strong as you.

GORDON: Don't, Nora. Don't always be cruel now.

NORA: I'm not cruel. It would be much crueller to keep you dangling around, puffed up with hope.

GORDON: I'd be happier.

NORA: Only for a bit. It couldn't go on.

GORDON: Why not?

NORA: Am I the kind of girl never to marry?

GORDON: Nora! You're not—not engaged?

NORA: Not—yet.

GORDON: But—when will it be, I wonder!

NORA: Now, you are rude. Couldn't I be engaged any minute I liked.

GORDON: Nora, how you tease me! And yet, I believe, underneath it all you are fond of me—a little.

NORA: Of course, I'm fond of you. We were brought up like brother and sister.

GORDON: But now, Nora—oh, bother!

(*There is a hullabaloo outside and* ROTO *and the* 1ST SHEPHERD *run on looking towards road and shouting*)

ROTO
1ST SHEP.: } Hey, mister, here's a sight. Look at that now! The first, the very first that's been along that road. Hoo-o!

(*There is the sound of a carefully driven car, and a spidery looking motor car driven by* VARLIE *draws up at the gate.* VARLIE *waves his hat.* ALL *run forward,* LOVEDAY *comes out of the house, the collie dog runs up, and a babble ensues*)

VARLIE: Yes, siree. I'm the boy to get the hustle on to these roads. I'll lay my bottom dollar this is the first car that has pulled up at this Homestead.

SEVERAL: Yes. It is. It is that. Just fancy!

NORA: I say, *what* an idea! You are a smart man, Mr. Varlie.

VARLIE: Smart! It 'ud tickle a racer to get ahead of me. I'm out to bring this country up to date. Why, you folk would go on sleeping here same as if automobiles had never been invented.

LOVEDAY: And I wish they hadn't!

VARLIE: You just say that, Miss Loveday, because you are a beautiful English girl—for England's so small it is most over-run with automobiles, that drop off it into the sea—but you wait till you see what this little roundabout can do for these God-forsaken stations.

GORDON: (*Grinning amiably*) Don't you lay it on too thick if you want to sell your car. And I suppose that's what you're after?

VARLIE: Sure! (*Laughing*) Did you think I was intending to give it to you?

GORDON: We might do without it.

VARLIE: Not likely. Not when you had once set eyes on it. The ladies would fair grab at it if you let it slip.

NORA: There is my dad—he'll be mad not to see it. He is away out in the hills, or I'd fetch him along this minute.

VARLIE: Waal, let me show you what this little packet of lightening can do. With this back seat raised she will take four of you into the city in just one-third of the time that your horses would take you on their backs. And you arrive spick and span as a daisy in your glad rags instead of carrying your things to change every time there is a dance or a theatre.

NORA: (*Clapping her hands*) Splendid, simply splendid. Wouldn't that be lovely!

LOVEDAY: It might.

GORDON: If it didn't jib half way.

VARLIE: No, siree. Not if you drive her right.

NORA: You'll have to learn how, Gordon.

GORDON: If *you* have the car I will learn to drive it all right.

NORA: I *must* have it.

GORDON: Your dad'll never spend so much just on your running about.

VARLIE: But I've not done yet, by gum! See what business she'll do. See what she will carry. If you don't have that little back seat raised, but have it locked down, this whole back top of her will open out on a hinge, and run behind on runners, stretching her out like a trolley car. See? (*He manipulates the back of car as he speaks*) Then you put up these rails, bolt 'em together—and look at the freight she'll carry!

NORA,
GORDON } Wonderful! I say, that's neat. Fancy that now!
and OTHERS } That's a difference from my young days.
TOGETHER:

VARLIE: She won't carry machinery or dead weight like that—but all your ordinary freight—flour, groceries—all you want out from the city—she'll take in your fruit so that you can sell it fresh in town instead of letting it rot on your trees—she—

GORDON: Have you sold any around here?

VARLIE: Sold any? Why, there's scarcely a station that isn't ordering one.

NORA: We must, dad *must*!

VARLIE: Ah, Miss Nora. I bet your poppa knows his duty to a peach like you!

GORDON: (*Prowls round the car, examining it closely and with interest*) Where was she made?

VARLIE: That's an Amurrican made sample, but when I have booked enough orders, the firm will set up and make them here.

GORDON: It is ingenious.

VARLIE: Any suggestion you like to make, sir, I'll report to my firm. We are out to supply to this country what she requires. It's a fresh, growing country with fresh-growing needs, and the firm that doesn't try to foist off continental models into it, but supplies those needs, will get some business.

GORDON: That is so.

VARLIE: Why, the folk around here don't know what it is to spend money. There's a power of unconscious demands right here waiting the supplies. You need to learn how to require luxuries.

GORDON: (*Hotly*) And waste good work making things we are happier without! No! Till this war is settled up, and after it, till everyone is fed and clothed decently, work must be spent on those jobs, not on senseless fripperies which enslave us to make some soulless idiot rich!

VARLIE: (*Strolls towards seat, down left*) Say! Have you got any lemonade? I'm as dry as a fish. (*Sits*)

(NORA and LOVEDAY *sit near him*)

GORDON: Here, Roto, fetch along the drinks! (ROTO *hurries into the house*)

1ST SHEP.: (*Hovering near car, to* GORDON) Eh! But it's a fair miracle. Boss!

GORDON: (*Leaving the car and coming to outskirts of group, down left*) Like all miracles, it don't seem *sure* to work.

(ROTO *returns, with tray of drinks and tumblers.* GORDON *helps to hand them round*)

GORDON: (*To* 1ST SHEPHERD, *stretching out with a tumbler towards him*) Here you are.

1ST SHEP.: Thank you, Boss. (*Comes up to outskirts of group and stands there sipping his drink*)

VARLIE: (*Cheerily*) Waal, and how have you been making time fly since I was here last?

NORA: Much as usual, only we work harder and—(*laughs*)—Gordon moons more than ever now he has someone to encourage him!

VARLIE: Ah, writes poetry, does he, poor chap?

GORDON: No. I don't.

NORA: Well, what you do is just as useless.

LOVEDAY: It isn't! He is working out ideas of great practical use—immense—there is nothing more important in the world.

VARLIE: So *that's* how the land lies! (*Twinkling a knowing look at* LOVEDAY's *unconscious face*) And what *is* the great idea, if I don't intrude?

GORDON: It is to make another such war as this impossible.

VARLIE: Oh, ho! That's a *real* smart idea, that is! Are you going to do it by preaching to the armies, or lovin' 'em like brothers, or how?

(ROTO *and* 1st SHEPHERD *guffaw loudly*)

GORDON: I'm no silly mug of a pacifist.

NORA: Their idea—

LOVEDAY: *His* idea—

NORA: Well then, as you like—his idea is to have only one army in the world. Ha, ha, ha. He, he, he! Isn't that practical!

LOVEDAY: Nora, you *are* a tease! It's nothing of the sort, Mr. Varlie. Gordon's idea is to have an international parliament, a super-parliament, and for that to have complete control of an international army, and also—what is very important—complete control of all armament making.

GORDON: Then any nation would have all the rest of the world against it directly it tried to do anything aggressive.

LOVEDAY: Yes. That's where it will get Germany so splendidly. Germany *pretends* she goes in for her militarism only for self-preservation. Now this international scheme will secure her self-preservation, but will entirely destroy her militarism and make her aggression impossible!

VARLIE: Donnerwetter! (*Confused, trying to cover his mistake*) Sake's alive—

NORA: (*Pertly*) Are *you* a German?

VARLIE: What do you take me for? I'm Amurrican. But I've travelled in Germany, like most travellers.

NORA: It would be a joke if you were a German, wouldn't it?

VARLIE: (*Cheerfully*) I'd be taking risks, wouldn't I? But let's hear more of this idea. It's a great idea if it'll kill German militarism! Why (*looking at* GORDON), I'd no idea you were such a top hole genius.

LOVEDAY: Now you're laughing, too. None of you seem to think war *can* be made impossible.

ROTO: That it can't, Missy. Not while men are men.

1ST SHEP.: (*Agreeing*) That's so, that's so!

LOVEDAY: How can *you* think that, Roto? Why, there used to be war in this very land between you and the English, and now there is none.

ROTO: That's because the Pakeha are strong. They make laws we have to obey. If a Maori kill a Pakeha or a Maori now, the Maori is hung by the law. So Maori and Pakeha live without killing.

LOVEDAY: But that's just it! If the International Parliament was strong and it made laws, the nations would have to obey and if one nation went to war and tried to kill another, that nation would suffer. So the nations would live without war.

1ST SHEP.: (*Shaking his head*) He, he, he! That's likely! (*Whistles to the collie and goes off*)

VARLIE: Germany would never consent.

GORDON: Then she would openly proclaim that her militarism is aggressive and not for self-defence. It would have to be one of the terms of peace that she did come in.

VARLIE: Waal, that may not be so easy.

LOVEDAY: Then all the more need for Gordon's scheme. It is the only way to destroy militarism.

GORDON: Without some such plan the nations will all be burdened beyond endurance, with armament making and the upkeep of armies.

LOVEDAY: And all the lovely face of England will be scarred with factories and works, and her people go grey and weary under roofs instead of singing while they work under the blue sky. And not only in England but everywhere, machines, machines, machines will sap the vitals of men and women and make life a grey and sordid fear!

NORA: Aren't they just *too* absurd for anything, those two! As though it was *their* business to set the world right!

GORDON: Whose is it then?

NORA: Nobody's.

GORDON: It is the business of everyone to make the world safer and more beautiful—

NORA: (*Putting her fingers in her ears*) Aren't they hopeless! (*To* VARLIE) Come along, and I'll show you my bed of English roses. You'll like them.

VARLIE: (*Rises, throws down a nearly burnt cigar and goes with her across stage, standing down right with her to admire a rose bed in bloom*) I guess you're the best rose among them all.

NORA: (*Smiles as if pleased*) You have nothing to sell *me*!

VARLIE: No. But I might have something to give.

(*Meanwhile* GORDON *limps off after smiling at* LOVEDAY. *She picks up a book and begins to read*)

NORA: *You* never give anything unless you get its value back!

VARLIE: This time it is a free gift I'm thinking of, but I don't deny I might get its value back! More than its value perhaps.

NORA: Well, I'm sure you haven't got anything I want as a gift.

VARLIE: Ah, you Angel face. Couldn't you take a free gift of a man?

NORA: What man?

VARLIE: Suppose it was myself!

NORA: (*Meditating*) You are a *man*.

VARLIE: I am that. Would you take me as a free gift?

NORA: But what would I do with you?

VARLIE: Waal—what does a woman do with a man? Sometimes she marries him.

NORA: Oh! Well—but *that* wouldn't be a free gift of a man. You would get me in exchange.

VARLIE: Didn't I say I might get more than its value back for my gift?

(*Meanwhile* ROTO *is sitting on the ground not far from* LOVEDAY, *finishing* VARLIE's *cigar, and playing with a carved jade curio. Between the puffs of the cigar, and under his breath, he hums snatches of the following song:*

[ROTO: *He roa te wa ki Tipirere*
*He tino mamao,*
*He roa te wa ki Tipirere,*
*Ki taku kotiro.*
*E noho pikatiri,*
*Hei kona rehita koea,*
*He mamao rawa Tipirere*
*Ka tae ahua.*])

NORA: Then that's no bargain for me!

VARLIE: Say, you think it over. I've got a mighty fine business now, and you could help me in it. You could live in the city or run about with me or whatever you liked—and say, Angel face, I think you are just the best ever!

NORA: You're smart—but—

VARLIE: (*Leans over quickly and kisses her*) Say, Angel face, that's a man's kiss, ain't it?

NORA: Oh! (*Confused, half pleased, half indignant*) That's not how to treat New Zealand girls! (*She runs into house and slams the door*)

(VARLIE, *satisfied with himself, strolls back across stage and stands looking down at the green jade curio* ROTO *is cleaning carefully.* LOVEDAY *continues to read near by*)

VARLIE: Say, Sambo, what's that pretty thing?

ROTO: I'm not a Sambo.

VARLIE: That's right. I beg yours.

ROTO: (*Resentfully*) My name's Roto, and I thought you knew it, Boss.

VARLIE: I did, then I didn't, and I do now. Waal, Roto, let's get back to the trail. What's that? (*Seats himself so that he can see the curio in* ROTO's *hands*)

ROTO: That's a hei-tiki.

VARLIE: A hei-tiki, is it? Does it tick?

ROTO: Silly joke. Hei-tiki is Maori.

VARLIE: What for?

ROTO: For this. (*Shows greenstone charm round his neck*) Same here.

VARLIE: Let me see.

ROTO: No. No one touch but me. It is tapu.

VARLIE: Tapu? What does that mean?

ROTO: No one may touch but me. This one is tapu, sacred.

VARLIE: I won't hurt it.

ROTO: When tapu put on anything, no one can touch unless tapu is raised.

VARLIE: Waal, and how is the tapu raised?

ROTO: Long ago, only death did—now—oh now, in weak men's time—*money* will raise tapu.

VARLIE: The almighty dollar! And how much money will raise this tapu?

ROTO: Much, very much.

VARLIE: Why?

Roto: This very rare, very useful hei-tiki.

Varlie: How so?

Roto: It has death in it, secret, strong death.

(Loveday *looks up from her reading and watches quietly, and with simple curiosity*)

Varlie: How?

Roto: Great secret. A very great wise chief found how to get secret poison from karaka kernels.

Varlie: Karaka?

Roto: Every New Zealand Pakeha knows karaka seeds, very bad poison. But kills too quick, too ugly, legs all stiff anyhow— all know that karaka poison. But this great chief took part of karaka seed-poison, mixed with magic, and then it kills more slowly in one, two hours after, like as if the man died of himself.

Varlie: And who do *you* want to kill?

Roto: Me? No fellow. All friends. But this hei-tiki useful. It has secret poison, no doctor could tell was poison. That's why tapu would cost much for a pakeha to touch it.

Varlie: I'd like to have it. How much?

Roto: Good Maori-stone carved hei-tiki, with secret death. Very much cost.

Varlie: Twenty shillings?

Roto: Oh, no, no! Two hundred shillings.

Varlie: Gosh! Let me see it.

Roto: No.

Varlie: Waal, you can't get my bottom dollar for a thing I haven't even seen!

Roto: (*Holds it carefully in his hands*) Well, see.

(*The audience also can see a green jade carving of very peculiar shape*)

Varlie: Where is the poison?

Roto: Quite safe. Inside. If top pressed hard, pushes bottom on one side, and poison drops out.

Varlie: Is the poison coloured?

Roto: Three or four drops clear like water. One drop enough. Try! And take the poison yourself!

Varlie: You old scamp. I guess you are not friends with me. You'd like me to take the poison!

Roto: (*Cunningly*) You're not deep friend to our Pakeha, are you?

VARLIE: (*Laughing noisily*) That's a good one! (*Looks up and sees* LOVEDAY) Say, Miss Loveday, did you hear that? He don't seem to trust me!

LOVEDAY: He has queer intuitions sometimes. But perhaps he is only afraid of your business superiority.

ROTO: Very cheap, Maori-stone, safe kill, no pakeha doctor could tell.

VARLIE: (*Laughing*) He's a nice villain!

LOVEDAY: He's all right. If he wanted to use it he wouldn't talk about it.

VARLIE: You're smart. Do you believe in it? Or is he just pulling my leg?

LOVEDAY: I believe in it. Gordon knows about a thing like that. I thought he said it was the last though.

ROTO: This the *very* last. This worth much money.

VARLIE: (*Taking out a pocketful of money*) Come. I'll have it, to keep you out of mischief. Take twenty shillings?

ROTO: No.

VARLIE: Forty then?

ROTO: No.

VARLIE: Fifty then? (*Lays out the money temptingly*)

ROTO: (*Looks eagerly at it, then yields*) Ten more.

VARLIE: Oh, all right! (*Lays down money*)

(ROTO *takes up the money, and hands the green stone to* VARLIE *who looks at it* (*so that audience can see its shape*) *then slips it into his pocket*)

VARLIE: (*Laughing reassuringly and sitting a little nearer* LOVEDAY) These queer old curios get me every time. I'll test a drop of his precious poison on a mangy old dog I have, and if it *is* as he says, I'll wash it out and keep eau de cologne in it. The jade is a pretty shape.

LOVEDAY: Yes, it is. And it is quite a good bit of jade, too. It is worth money. But do be careful with the stuff. I more than half believe what he says.

VARLIE: An old hand like I am at life, don't run no risks with a bit of jade. I've seen too much of the world.

LOVEDAY: You have travelled much?

VARLIE: I should say! I have run around a bit, and got into many a good scrape in my time. Why, any day you are lonesome, Miss Loveday, ask me for the story of my wounds!

LOVEDAY: I've been rather lonesome this afternoon. How did you get that red triangle on your right cheek bone? I have often wondered. It is so regular.

VARLIE: (*Turns his right cheek so that she can see it, points it out and turns again so that audience can see the bright red, definite small triangle on his cheek*) Ah, now that's one of my best stories. I was a spry young fellow then. (*Looks at her*) Now, if you were a smart girl you'd say, "*That's* not long ago then, Mr. Varlie!"

LOVEDAY: (*Smiling*) I'll say it if it is a regulation part of the story. Is it?

VARLIE: Waal, as you are a high and mighty young English girl, we'll take it as said.

(*Sounds of footsteps and panting along road*—1ST SHEPHERD *hurries on carrying a telegram held out before him*)

1ST SHEP.: Where's Mr. Gordon? Oh, where is he? This telegram's for him.

LOVEDAY: He went round the back of the house not long ago.

1ST SHEP.: Oh, terrible, terrible. That I've to take him this telegram.

LOVEDAY: What is it?

1ST SHEP.: Bad news, terrible bad news. The postman, he told me.

LOVEDAY: (*Anxiously*) But tell us.

1ST SHEP.: Oh, Missy, how'll ever Mister Gordon take it? Mr. Robert has been killed.

LOVEDAY: (*Sinking back in chair*) Robert *killed*, oh! *poor* Gordon!

VARLIE: Sakes alive, that's a knock out.

1ST SHEP.: That's what I say. It had better been the other way about.

LOVEDAY: (*Swiftly, in anger*) How *can* you say that?

NORA: (*Running out of house*) What *is* the fuss?

1ST SHEP.: (*A little important as being the bearer of sad news*) Ah, Missy, it's sad tidings there is in this telegram. Mr. Robert's killed.

NORA: (*Screams and staggers.* LOVEDAY *springs up and goes to her*) Robert, Robert! Killed. How do you know? It must be lies. How do you know?

1ST SHEP.: Postman told me. This is a Government telegram, telling it to ye, official.

GORDON: (*Hurries round the house and comes centre forward*) Whatever is the matter?

(ROTO *comes in and learning news from* VARLIE, *shows signs of real grief.*

All *hesitate to tell* Gordon. 1st Shepherd *holds out telegram*)

1st Shep.: It's, it's bad news, Mister Gordon.

Gordon: The telegram is official—it's—is Robert wounded? (*Tears open the telegram*)

Gordon: Killed! (*Lets telegram fall, and staggers forward to chair, all are silent*)

Nora: (*Crying softly*) Oh Robert, Robert, Robert!

(Loveday *tries to soothe her and is sad also.* Roto *sniffs. The collie dog comes up to the group, looking from one to the other, then goes to* Gordon *and rubs against him licking his hand.* Gordon *pats him*)

Gordon: Good old chap. Yes, he'll never come back. Your master is dead—died a hero's death.

Varlie: (*Comes up and shakes* Gordon's *hand*) Accept my condolences.

Gordon: Thanks—thanks, you're kind. (*Pays little attention to him, goes over to* Nora, *who is still weeping*) Nora, dear. (*He kneels beside her*) How sweet of you to care so much—he, he'd be proud if he knew.

Nora: (*Fiercely*) He wouldn't! He never cared for me. *And I loved him*—and I hate you. Go away!

(*She pushes him roughly from her so that, on his knees, still, he scarcely keeps his balance. She turns and weeps fiercely in* Loveday's *arms.* Loveday, *soothing her, really watches and feels for* Gordon. *As he staggers blindly to his feet, she looks with infinite tenderness and pity towards him and stretches out a hand to steady him. He takes it, and clasps it for a moment*)

Roto: (*Wailing*) What'll happen? What'll happen now Mister Robert won't come back?

1st Shep.: Eh, eh, dear, dear.

Gordon: He won't come back! (*He looks up suddenly, and seems to gather strength*) He won't come back! He has done *his* job for the Empire! That frees me! Now I'll do mine! I've nothing to keep me here.

1st Shep.: Why! the sheep do, Boss.

Gordon: Robert charged me to keep the station going for him till he came back. Now he'll never come back; I'm done with the station! Other men must raise the sheep.

Loveday: (*Her eyes sparkling*) You'll go to London?

Gordon: Yes. We have often said I'd have to go to London some day to get *my* job put through.

VARLIE: (*Half aside*) The man's mad! He doesn't propose seriously to bring forward that devilish scheme of his. (*Aloud*) What will you do? Have you the dollars? It'll take a good deal of money!

GORDON: No. All I have is the homestead, and the sheep. But I'll sell them.

VARLIE: It's the worst time to sell just now.

GORDON: I'll lose something of course, but the homestead and all is really worth quite ten thousand pounds altogether.

VARLIE: Snakes! It's not worth nearly half that.

1ST SHEP.: Yes it is, Mister. It's a good station. None better hereabouts.

VARLIE: Is it freehold?

GORDON: Yes. And unencumbered.

VARLIE: Is it all yours?

GORDON: Yes—*now* it is. Robert and I shared it. He left his will with me—he said his share was all for me, as he hadn't got a girl.

(NORA *is seen to shudder as though hurt*)

VARLIE: Then you can sell at once.

GORDON: I shall.

1ST SHEP.: Don't 'e, Mister Gordon, don't 'e. You'll best wait. Land's not sellin' just now. Wait a bit.

GORDON: But my work won't wait! I shan't.

LOVEDAY: Splendid! Go.

GORDON: You say so? You back me?

LOVEDAY: Yes. Yes.

GORDON: Well, I have one on my side.

VARLIE: It's a fool business.

GORDON: I must sell at once. Perhaps neighbour Lee might like to join this station on to his.

NORA: (*Looking up fiercely*) My dad? I won't let him. I won't!

VARLIE: You'll not get a purchaser at present.

ROTO: That's true, Boss. No one is buying land just now.

GORDON: (*Turning away*) Well, I must sell for else I have no money to go to Europe with and I *will* go. It will be a very expensive job. Propaganda costs. I must put my scheme before the Prime Minister of England, and it's no good to write to him. I must see him, I must talk to him.

VARLIE: Has he a good opinion of you?

GORDON: He doesn't know me yet.

NORA: (*Scolding*) How do you think that you, an absolutely unknown Colonial with a hair-brained scheme, are going to get at him?

GORDON: I'll manage it somehow.

VARLIE: London is not like Dunedin, I opine. Do you know anyone in London who knows the Prime Minister?

GORDON: No. But I'll get to.

NORA: Do you know a single living soul in London?

GORDON: No. But I will when I get there.

LOVEDAY: He will. *I'll* see to that!

NORA: (*Spitefully*) Oh! Do *you* know people who know the Prime Minister of England?

LOVEDAY: (*Quietly*) I do.

NORA: (*Taken aback*) Oh! Who?

LOVEDAY: The Duchess of Rainshire.

VARLIE: (*Very alert, evidently taking note of the name*) Does she know the Prime Minister intimately?

LOVEDAY: Yes. He often comes to see her.

GORDON: (*Triumphfully*) Splendid! You never told me that, Loveday, when you said I should have to go and see him somehow.

LOVEDAY: (*Smiling*) I had it up my sleeve though. There was no need to speak of it so long as you were not going. Now (*sadly*) you can think only of this work. I'll be proud to help in it. It is worth doing.

GORDON: With Robert's example before me—I'll do it, or die.

LOVEDAY: You'll do it.

GORDON: But it may take a long time, and I must have money, plenty of money too. I must sell the station at once.

VARLIE: (*Drawling*) I've put my thinking cap on. A business connection of my firm is looking out for freehold in this country. If this is freehold, I reckon I'd be safe to get my money back from him if I bought it myself.

GORDON: You!

VARLIE: Yaas. I've got plenty of free cash when it's wanted, you know. Business hasn't been bad lately, and—waal. I'll lay down for this freehold of yours.

GORDON: Good. That'll save ever so much time I might waste in looking for a buyer.

VARLIE: Let's strike then.

GORDON: It is worth ten thousand pounds.

VARLIE: Shucks!

GORDON: But I'll take less.

VARLIE: Waal?

GORDON: Say seven thousand—for money down.

VARLIE: (*Laughing derisively*) What do you take me for?

GORDON: It is really worth that, why the sheep alone—

VARLIE: Sell your sheep separately then. I ain't buying sheep, I'm buying land.

1ST SHEP.: But you can't do nothin' with this land without sheep, Boss.

ROTO: It's worth more than seven thousand pounds, that's a bargain price, Boss.

VARLIE: Sell elsewhere then.

ROTO: Do, Mister Gordon. Next month a Pakeha I know is coming to the city. He thinkin' of a station like this. I fetch him along, Mister Gordon.

GORDON: Next *month*! I want to be half way to England next month.

VARLIE: (*Lighting a cigar*) I'll give you four thousand five hundred for it—

GORDON: That's too little to discuss.

1ST SHEP.: That's robbery, Boss, don't take it. After the war it'll fetch three times that. After the war—

GORDON: After the war will be too late for me. The international super-parliament must be considered in the terms of peace.

1ST SHEP.: (*Groans*) Them ideas! You'd let the sheep rot for ideas!

VARLIE: I'll give you four thousand five hundred for it, down *today*.

GORDON: Today!

VARLIE: Right now. We'll ride into the city and get a notary to fix it up all square.

GORDON: That's better than waiting for an uncertain buyer—but it's very little—

VARLIE: But it's here, *today*.

GORDON: Today. Well, I'll take it!

VARLIE: Done. A deal. Shake.

(ROTO *and the* SHEPHERD *mutter, and shake their heads*)

NORA: You're a perfect *fool*, Gordon! You throw away more than half your fortune so as to be able to rush off to England with a crack-brained scheme! Why not write to the papers instead?

GORDON: (*Looks helpless, says appealingly*) Oh, Nora!

VARLIE: A lot of energy is let off safely in gas to the papers. Hyde is bottlin' his energy up it seems. That makes him dangerous, eh?

GORDON: (*To Loveday*) You'll give me a letter of introduction?

LOVEDAY: (*Smiling sweetly*) No. I won't.

VARLIE: Gee. Even *she* thinks you are going off the rails.

GORDON: Loveday, you *said* you would give me a letter of introduction!

LOVEDAY: How many introductory letters do you suppose the Duchess of Rainshire gets? A *letter* would do you very little good.

GORDON: (*Crestfallen*) Oh, Loveday, what do you mean?

LOVEDAY: Why! (*Taking a step towards him, radiant, in the centre of stage*) I'm not going to trust to letters, which people can put in the waste-paper basket!

GORDON: But, what do you mean, Loveday?

LOVEDAY: *I'll come with you myself!* I'll wait on their doorsteps (I know lots of people in London), I'll waylay them at parties, and seize the very *best* opportunities for getting the right people to know you.

GORDON: You will? You are a brick! How splendid!

VARLIE: (*Somewhat disturbed, aside*) Ach! The English are mad enough for anything. Gott sei dank I know of this! (*Aloud*) What about Mrs. Grundy?

NORA: Yes. A pretty pair you will look. What will people say?

LOVEDAY: When the whole world's future is at stake, do you think I care what people say?

VARLIE: Who was it said the English are all mad? He was right.

GORDON: It is too much, Loveday!

NORA: You are English. You will make me agree with Mr. Varlie's opinion of your country's sanity.

LOVEDAY: British women are free from the need to care what foolish people think! (*Turning to* GORDON) We will go to London, Gordon, and there I'll work for you and your great idea, for all I'm worth!

(GORDON *takes a step towards her, his face shining with enthusiasm*)

CURTAIN

MARIE STOPES

# Act III

*About a Couple of months later than Act II.*

*The Duchess of Rainshire's drawing-room, London. The fore-part of the stage represents an alcove of the big drawing-room; the back of the stage opens out so as to suggest a large room beyond. Heavy curtains hang on either side of back of alcove. Left second entrance, a door leading direct from alcove to outer hall. Left front, up against wall and projecting into room, a grand piano, closed. Right front, a large Chesterfield placed at convenient angle. One or two small chairs, big pictures, a palm or two, etc., as in a first class house.*

THE DUCHESS OF RAINSHIRE, LOVEDAY *and* GORDON *DISCOVERED in the foreground. Back of stage occasional guests pass to and fro in the big drawing-room, and faint sounds of music in the distance are heard.*

THE DUCHESS *is a middle-aged, smart woman of the world, with a commanding manner and quick way of speaking, but kindly.*

GORDON: (*Standing, speaking earnestly declaiming as though concluding a long argument*) I fear I have bored you, there is so much to say, but perhaps the chief point is that there shall not only be international law, but adequate force behind that law to enforce it.

DUCHESS: (*Stifling a yawn*) Well, Mr. Hyde, I'm sure I wish you the success you deserve, and not what I fear you are likely to get. London simply swarms with panaceas and their parents.

LOVEDAY: (*Appealing*) But they haven't all got *you* to help them!

DUCHESS: Oh yes, most of them have! But mercifully the schemes counteract each other on the whole, or where should *I* be?

LOVEDAY: You must not allow *anything* to counteract this.

DUCHESS: (*To* MR. HYDE) Well, young man, remember! It's neither for yourself nor for your ideas I'm launching you on the defenceless man at the helm, but simply because Loveday used to have fascinating freckles on her nose when she was six years old.

GORDON: I know I owe her an awful lot. And you too. I'm ever so grateful, I can't say how grateful. Posterity will—

DUCHESS: (*Interrupting*) You are going to say that I'll go down to history as the patron of genius, of course—I'm glad to hear it. It may help to counteract the *other* way I shall go down to history. No one who has had two successive husbands, both Dukes, could fail to find posterity as critical as the present generation is spiteful.

(GORDON *looks bewildered*)

LOVEDAY: Don't believe her, Gordon. Everybody's awfully fond of her.

DUCHESS: Go and think that over somewhere by yourself, young man. I haven't seen Loveday since her escapade into Greater Britain and I want to hear from her how this little island looks in true prospective.

(GORDON *bows and goes toward back of stage and mingles with other quests, strolling out of sight. Meanwhile a guest or two stroll partly round the alcove, but seeing the* DUCHESS *talking, retire*)

DUCHESS: (*Taking* LOVEDAY's *arm and pushing her down on to sofa, sits beside her*) Now, Miss, your confessions.

LOVEDAY: He is really wonderful.

DUCHESS: Though New Zealand is British my experience of home Britons tells me it is not peopled by geniuses. He is exceptional. Naturally.

LOVEDAY: Not at all naturally.

DUCHESS: Hoity-toity.—I'm not old enough to say that properly, but it is so effective, I'm beginning young, so as to get enough practice before my public use of it. So—hoity-toity!

(LOVEDAY *smiles, says nothing*)

DUCHESS: What's wrong, don't I say it properly? It ought to elicit some retort from you which should reveal your secret more completely than ever.

LOVEDAY: I haven't got a secret.

DUCHESS: Hoity-toity!—I think I did it rather better that time—

LOVEDAY: (*Earnestly*) I *haven't* a secret really!

DUCHESS: I must have done it better: you retorted, telling me that you have a secret.

LOVEDAY: (*Laughing*) I haven't, really and truly I haven't.

DUCHESS: Hoit—no. I'll vary it. Fiddlesticks! Who is it?

LOVEDAY: *Who* is what?

DUCHESS: Whom are you in love with?

LOVEDAY: Nobody.

DUCHESS: Is he in love with you?

LOVEDAY: Who? Nobody? Yes. Nobody is in love with me.

DUCHESS: He. (*Points with her fan through opening of alcove*) Your New Zealand Genius.

LOVEDAY: (*A shade despondently, but unconscious of it*) No, he is not.

DUCHESS: (*Pouncing*) Ha! that's it, is it?

LOVEDAY: That's what? Oh, dear! Why is it I always talk such bad English when I am with you?

DUCHESS: Tush. Tell me about him!

LOVEDAY: (*Brightening*) Oh, how nice of you. I did *so* want you to take an interest in his ideas. They are so *wonderful*. They will make—

DUCHESS: I don't care one Jellicoed submarine about his ideas. Tell me about himself.

LOVEDAY: He is a little lame, poor boy—

DUCHESS: So I *have* observed.

LOVEDAY: But it isn't fundamental. He got a stake through his thigh when he was a lad and it healed badly. It must have been dreadful for him.

DUCHESS: Are you going to marry him?

LOVEDAY: Oh, how *can* you say such things? It has never entered his head!

DUCHESS: Hoity-toity.

LOVEDAY: Oh, it hasn't!

DUCHESS: Well, here is a personable young man for whom you feel pity, and you are twenty-seven to his thirty. I only ask, are you going to marry him?

LOVEDAY: (*Rising indignantly*) How *can* you say such things. I never thought of it! Why he—he loves someone else!

DUCHESS: Oh, *that's* the trouble, is it? Where is she?

LOVEDAY: In New Zealand.

DUCHESS: (*Patting* LOVEDAY's *hand*) Then that's all right, my dear. You can have him if you want.

LOVEDAY: But I don't want, that way.—Oh, I don't want any way! Oh, why *do* you have such dreadful conversations?

DUCHESS: That's it. Quarrel with your benefactor! Are you going to flounce out of the house *before* the Prime Minister comes?

LOVEDAY: I can't now—but I'm not going to take anything back because you promised to help us.

DUCHESS: (*Laughing delightedly and pulling* LOVEDAY *down again beside her*) Oh, so it is us?

LOVEDAY: Only for this piece of work, till his idea is launched, of course. What do you suppose I came across from New Zealand for?

DUCHESS: (*Chuckling*) I wondered.

LOVEDAY: Don't you care a bit for a big idea that will help the world? Can't you imagine a woman gladly crossing the world to have even a small share in helping it forward?

DUCHESS: I could imagine it; but I have never yet *observed* it.

LOVEDAY: Well, you can now. Look at me.

DUCHESS: I do, my child, and I see a young woman in love.

LOVEDAY: (*Shaking herself*) Ooh!

DUCHESS: Never mind, my dear. He is a personable young man enough. There are no available Dukes, Earls or Marquises I can recommend at present and I believe in people marrying for love. I have seen too much of the other thing. So what can I do for you?

LOVEDAY: You know quite well. I only asked you, begged you, to make the Prime Minister listen to him.

DUCHESS: Oh, the poor man! When he comes here for an hour it is for relaxation and quiet. He looks to me to *protect* him from Cranks, not to stuff them down his throat.

LOVEDAY: (*Emphatically*) Gordon is *not* a crank.

DUCHESS: All cranks have emphatic relatives who testify ardently to their sanity.

LOVEDAY: I'm *not* his relative.

DUCHESS: Hoity-toity.

LOVEDAY: (*Smiling*) That doesn't react with me any longer. (*Coaxing*) Come now, be an *angel* and introduce Gordon to the Prime Minister. Don't say anything about your suspicions that he is a crank. Just say he is a nice young man from New Zealand.

DUCHESS: And what am I to say about you? Or are you dying to be sacrificed on the altar of friendship and have nothing said about you?

LOVEDAY: Oh, yes.

DUCHESS: You don't insist on an introduction too?

LOVEDAY: No. I ask only one introduction. Promise *that*.

DUCHESS: Very well.

LOVEDAY: You darling!

DUCHESS: But I will use the introduction for you, not the man. The Prime Minister likes young girls if they are at all good looking, and I think one may call you that.

LOVEDAY: Oh, you mustn't! I *won't* be introduced.

DUCHESS: What! You refuse to be introduced to the Prime Minister?

LOVEDAY: (*Punching a cushion*) I do. I do absolutely. That one introduction is for Gordon. You *promised* one; and Gordon is to have it.

(*The* REV. DR. VARLIE, *separating himself from the guests, has strolled into the alcove*)

DUCHESS: Well, I suppose it must be.

LOVEDAY: You are a *dear*.

DUCHESS: But for your purpose, it is not the Prime Minister you want first of all. There is another Cabinet Minister whose word in the Prime Minister's ear would be priceless.

LOVEDAY: Oh! Then *please* introduce Gordon to him first!

DUCHESS: He's very amiable.

LOVEDAY: Splendid. Is he here tonight?

DUCHESS: Yes. Go and fetch your phenomenon. If you two are to be found here when wanted. I'll either send for you or stroll this way with him if I can.

LOVEDAY: Thanks *awfully*! (*Goes through curtains, to drawing-room beyond*)

(*The* REV. DR. VARLIE *advances. He has a considerable beard, and wears clerical garb. He politely presents himself to the Duchess. She greets him without enthusiasm*)

DUCHESS: Oh, Dr. Chapman, I'm glad you found time to come for a little relaxation.

VARLIE: Oh, dear lady. I take no relaxation in these sad times. But I wanted a word with you before your next Committee for the relief of the homeless Serbians. As you know, the American people have been stirred to the depths, and out of the fulness of their hearts they have sent *me* to join my ministrations with yours. As you well know, these weeks past I have put my back into it.

DUCHESS: Very good of you I'm sure. We can't have too much help. *Practical* help.

VARLIE: At the last Committee Meeting I opined that a cheque would not be out of place in your hands, Duchess.

DUCHESS: Never.

VARLIE: (*Taking out his pocket book*) Waal, my flock answered my prayers, and sent this to me for you. If you could sign the receipt yourself, Duchess, it would be like placing seed in fertile ground. I know your secretary does such routine work for you, Duchess, and that's why I took this chance of handing it to you myself.

DUCHESS: Of course I'll sign the receipt if you like. Is that all?

VARLIE: Waal, the other business will do when we meet at the next Committee.

DUCHESS: (*Moving off, back of stage*) Then come along with me, and I'll find you an interesting girl or two to entertain you. You just missed one as you came in.

VARLIE: So I divined from her earnestness. A lovely type.

(*They go out together. In a moment* LOVEDAY *and* GORDON *return*)

LOVEDAY: So we are to sit *here* till she comes or sends for you.

GORDON: (*Gratefully*) I *say*. You do work miracles.

LOVEDAY: It is the Duchess who will do that. Isn't she a dear?

GORDON: She terrifies me rather.

LOVEDAY: For moments, just at times, she terrifies me. But all the safe times in between I know she is a dear.

GORDON: I say, I'm nervous you know.

LOVEDAY: Oh, *don't* be! You will only have a few minutes this time: just to make a good impression. If you do that then the Minister may give you a serious interview later.

GORDON: I'm wretchedly nervous. Is he, is he *short* with people?

LOVEDAY: He likes people to be short with him! He is dreadfully bored by long-winded cranks of course.

GORDON: I say, what do you think? (*Pulls out some papers from his pocket*) I thought of wording Clause 29 of the suggested constitution as follows: "The Super-Parliament is to have the power of prohibiting the manufacture of *anything* which in its opinion constitutes a menace to the Peace of the world: with power to inflict the death penalty on all concerned in any infringement of its prohibition in any country."

LOVEDAY: Yes. I think that is good. Coupled with the other clauses that makes it safer.

GORDON: I hope the Prime Minister will see that. I must learn this clause off by heart now. Teach it to me, will you?

LOVEDAY: You don't know the other clauses off by heart, *do* you?

GORDON: Yes, of course I learnt them. I couldn't *read* them to the Prime Minister, could I? And I'm so nervous, I'd muddle them up unless I just learn them off.

LOVEDAY: (*Horrified*) You don't intend to *say off* all the thirty-three clauses of the suggested constitution to the Prime Minister at this first meeting, do you?

GORDON: (*Simply surprised*) Why, yes! I'm to tell him the ideas, aren't I?

LOVEDAY: Good heavens! not in a block like that though. After you have made an impression on him you must give him these all typed out so that his secretaries and colleagues and everybody can make marginal notes on them and hash them up.

GORDON: If I'm not to say the clauses I have learnt, what on earth *am* I to say?

LOVEDAY: Say you have an idea worth his serious attention—say—oh—whatever he makes you *feel* will reach his attention!

GORDON: Good heavens. What a gamble!

LOVEDAY: Not a bit. The inspiration will come.

GORDON: *You* have been my inspiration for so much of this.

LOVEDAY: No, no. I have only suggested a word here and there.

GORDON: I owe you so much. How strange it is I should have met you the same day that the vision came to me. Next to my vision-spirit, you are the source of all the ideas worth anything in it.

LOVEDAY: Nonsense. Absolute nonsense. I simply had nothing concrete in my mind at first! It is you, you, *you* who have put all the ideas into practical, living, useful shape.

GORDON: But *I* had no concrete ideas at first!

LOVEDAY: Well, *you* evolved them out of your inner consciousness.

GORDON: (*Obstinately*) The vision, and you, gave me the ideas to work out.

LOVEDAY: (*Almost irritably*) It's sheer *nonsense*, that old vision! The thoughts were yours, yours, *yours*! She only mumbled a little vague *tosh*!

GORDON: (*Astonished*) Loveday!

LOVEDAY: Well, I'm tired of seeing you being so humble, and failing to realise how splendid you are, and how the credit of it is all your *own*.

GORDON: Loveday.—You don't really think that?

LOVEDAY: I do.

GORDON: (*Whimsically*) I'm so accustomed to women thinking poorly of me—Nora—

LOVEDAY: (*After a pause*) Does she—does she still *hurt* you, Gordon?

GORDON: No I have waked from my foolish dream of love for her. She, she was too cruel—and besides—she, you know, you heard—she loved Robert.

LOVEDAY: (*Joy showing in her face, which she tries to conceal*) Then you
feel free.

GORDON: Yes. Thank God I'm free from love of any earthly woman.

(LOVEDAY'S *face falls*)

GORDON: *You* make most women look small, and then—then—anyway,
I'm not the type of man such a woman as I could love now, would look
at. Thank God, no mortal woman can rack my heart. My vision Queen
has my heart and my dreams.

(LOVEDAY *looks bright—then a little mischievous.* VARLIE *returns,
strolling round the room, unnoticed by them. He starts somewhat at seeing
them talking together so deeply and nods as if recognising something and
saying "ha ha" to himself. He studies the angle of the room and places
himself back of the piano, turning towards the wall and pretending
to examine a picture. Meanwhile* LOVEDAY *and* GORDON *continue,
unaware, to talk*)

LOVEDAY: Spirits *don't* appear. She must have been a real woman.

GORDON: Impossible.

LOVEDAY: But a spirit is *more* impossible! (*triumphantly*) So you see,
every single bit of credit for it is yours.

GORDON: Yours.

(*Both laughing say together "yours."*)

(*From back of stage, enter* CABINET MINISTER *with the* DUCHESS. *THE*
MINISTER *is old, benign and white haired, with a long white beard. A
plain clothes detective* (SMITHERS) *in evening dress follows him at a little
distance and hovers near the curtains at the back*)

MINISTER: Ah! I remembered that this alcove is generally nice and
quiet. You are a good hostess, my dear.

(*The* DUCHESS *throws a comical look at the back of the sofa where* GORDON
*and* LOVEDAY *are sitting*)

DUCHESS: I'm glad *you* think so! It isn't easy to satisfy different people
at the same time.

MINISTER: All I ask is a quiet cup of coffee with you, my dear. Can
we have some coffee here, by the way?

DUCHESS: Of course. (*Slips quickly to wall and rings*) It will be here
directly.

MINISTER: And your coffee is good. Ah, it reminds me of Paris
in the late seventies—when I was a young man. But you didn't
know Paris in the late seventies I expect? No, no, of course not.

(MAID *in smart uniform, waistcoat, brass buttons, enters from entrance right, going quickly up to the* DUCHESS, *who whispers "coffee at once, here."* MAID *goes out*)

MINISTER: Paris in the seventies was an adventure.

DUCHESS: Any city is an adventure to the right man.

(MAID *enters with coffee,* MINISTER *helps himself to sugar and cream, stands centre of stage holding it in his hand*)

MINISTER: That's true. You are a witty woman, my dear. And that's a thing not often come by now-a-days.

DUCHESS: Modern women are all clever, and cleverness kills wit as a magnifying glass kills a complexion.

MINISTER: Good, good.

(LOVEDAY *and* GORDON, *observing their nearness, rise and stand a little way off. The* DUCHESS *signals imperiously to* LOVEDAY, *but she makes a determined grimace and slips round the left side of the sofa. As she leaves* GORDON *she whispers "The great moment is coming—Good Luck."* GORDON *stands hesitating. The* DUCHESS *signs to him to come forward*)

DUCHESS: Ah, *here* is the young man of whom I spoke to you. May I introduce Mr. Hyde? You said you could endure a chat with him. He wants your influence with the Prime Minister you know. I tell him *you* are even more important.

MINISTER: Flatterer!

(LOVEDAY *behind the group waves her hand joyously.* HYDE *looks relieved and very pleased*)

DUCHESS: The power behind the throne, Mr. Hyde.

MINISTER: (*Kindly*) Ah, how do you do, Mr. Hyde.

(*Shakes hands after carefully turning and laying down his coffee cup on the corner of the piano behind him, placing the cup so that it is on the audience side of the piano.* VARLIE, *who is still standing with his back to the group, looking at the picture above the piano, notes this quickly and keenly. He is seen by the audience to be listening intently*)

MINISTER: How do you do. You come from Australia I believe?

GORDON: New Zealand, Sir.

MINISTER: New Zealand, yes, yes. A thousand miles by sea from the nearest port in Australia.

GORDON: Yes, Sir.

MINISTER: I remember that because I was there myself when I was a young man and very much it surprised me to be sure. I had always pictured New Zealand as being to Australia like England to the Continent. Yes, yes. A thousand miles away. Just think what a difference it would make, if *England* were a thousand miles from France at this present moment.

GORDON: Yes indeed, Sir.

MINISTER: So it is very fine of you young New Zealanders to join in with us all the way you do. Very fine.

(LOVEDAY *crosses to right of stage and looks curiously at* VARLIE *but without recognition*)

GORDON: We are Britons all, Sir.

MINISTER: Yes, yes. We are all fighting shoulder to shoulder, though I expect the realisation of it has hardly touched you yet.

GORDON: My only brother was killed a few weeks ago in Gallipoli, Sir.

MINISTER: Dear, dear. A sad business that. I'm sorry for that, my lad.

GORDON: (*Beginning to be desperate*) And that is one reason why, Sir, I am so anxious to ask your help for my scheme of international—

(VARLIE *meanwhile has very quietly slipped round so as to be on the front of the piano, within reach of coffee cup*)

MINISTER: (*Putting up his hand and gently interrupting*) Now don't talk about schemes, young man. This is my recreation hour. Seeing you carries me back to when I was a young chap myself. My father was one of the old school and sent me round the world to finish my education.

(VARLIE'S *right cheek now faces* LOVEDAY, *she gazes at it, starts with amazed half recognition, for the top half of the scar is visible*)

MINISTER: I remember very well going to New Zealand—and seeing its pink and white terraces. Ah! They were wonderful, wonderful.

GORDON: They must have been, Sir (*his heart beginning to sink into his boots*)

MINISTER: Yes, of course. They were destroyed before you could have seen them. A terrible volcanic outburst that! Incredible. Why those great pink and white terraces looked as though no power on earth could destroy them. So beautiful they were too! So beautiful. Like coloured marble that had been spun into lace cascades by magicians. Well, well, *sic transit gloria mundi*! (*He shakes* GORDON's *hand*) I'm glad to have had this little talk with you, Mr. Hyde. These pleasant meetings help to link up the Empire. Good-bye. Good Luck.

*(Meanwhile, through the last part of this conversation,* VARLIE *has taken out the Green Jade Carving, seen in Act II, from his pocket.* LOVEDAY *recognises it and shows tense anxiety and suppressed excitement.* VARLIE *glances stealthily round the room, and sees that no one is looking at him, for* LOVEDAY *pretends not to see him; she then turns her head just in time to see him drop a drop of the poison into the coffee cup on the piano, and quickly to turn away, his back to the group, and go to another picture, hanging down right front of the piano.* VARLIE *calmly pretends to be absorbed in examining the picture.* LOVEDAY *is for a moment weak with amazement and anxiety, and is evidently hesitating as to what course to follow, by the time the* MINISTER *says, "Good-bye, good luck.")*

GORDON: Good-bye, Sir, thank you. (*Desperate*) And may I come and see you in office hours about my scheme? It is very important, it—is a series of clauses for an international arrangement which will wipe German Militarism and all other militarism off the earth—it—

MINISTER: If you *must* send it—and I really ask you not to, I am deluged with other people's ideas—if you *must* send it, my secretary will attend to it. Good-bye.

*(*GORDON *steps back very dejected. The* MINISTER *turns, takes up his coffee cup and says a word to the* DUCHESS*)*

MINISTER: And now for our chat, my dear.

*(He raises the coffee cup, about to drink slowly.* LOVEDAY *springs forward and dashes the cup from his hand, spilling the coffee.* [NOTE.—*Better have a brown carpet so that the successive stains of a long run won't show*] *The* DUCHESS *and* MINISTER *look amazed)*

LOVEDAY: (*Panting but quietly*) That man, that man there!

*(Points at* VARLIE, *who is now in the corner between the footlights, the piano, and the* MINISTER'S *group. Very unostentatiously he digs the jade piece into the earth of pot and has barely covered it by this time)*

Hold him, Gordon, hold him.

*(*GORDON *literally hurls himself on* VARLIE *and, before he has time to turn, has his two arms pinned from behind. The two men struggle. The* MINISTER *looks bewildered. Hearing the struggle the evening-dress-clad detective near the curtains comes forward hurriedly and helps* GORDON. *They succeed in holding* VARLIE*)*

DUCHESS: For God's sake don't have a scene in public.

*(She runs across room and rings repeatedly.* MAID *comes in by door right)*

DUCHESS: (*To* MAID) Draw those curtains *instantly* and stand by
them. Don't let anyone in, not anyone unless I tell you.

(*The* MAID *hurries to obey and draws the heavy velvet curtains, shutting off
the alcove from the main drawing room and stations herself by them*)

MINISTER: Dear, dear, what *is* this all about! Why it is a clergyman!
isn't it? What on earth are they handling a clergyman in this
fashion for? Why, Smithers man, you are to guard me, not to assist
a young ruffian in mauling a reverend gentleman.

SMITHERS: (*Puzzled, half relaxing hold on* VARLIE) I'm sure, Sir, I don't
know—

LOVEDAY: Don't, *don't* leave him! For God's sake hold him.

DUCHESS: What *on earth* is this outrageous fracas about? Loveday, I'm
*amazed*! The Rev. Dr. Chapman is an American whom I know and
respect. Let him go at once, Smithers. And you, Mr. Hyde, you
outrageous humbug!

LOVEDAY: Don't! (*She goes quickly up to* VARLIE, *pulls his beard with one
hand, and it comes off*)

(*Amazement and consternation of all*)

LOVEDAY: Yes, I thought so! Look, Gordon, see that scar on his cheek,
that little triangular red scar! But anyway you must know his face
now, it is VARLIE!

VARLIE: How the devil—What does all this mean! You attack the
Minister of Peace! I am the Rev. Dr. Chapman, as you well know,
Duchess. If I choose to wear a false beard till my own grows
because I desire to follow John the Baptist's example, though alas
late in life, is *that* any crime? Why don't you go round among
your guests and arrest the ladies with false hair. *They* intend
to attract and deceive while I but symbolise my belief in the
Nazarene vows.

(*He seems to be making an impression on the* DUCHESS *and the* MINISTER)

LOVEDAY: No! Hold him, he's dangerous. Hold him till I can tell you
all!

GORDON: Sure, Loveday, *I'll* hold him, even if Mr. Smithers won't.

LOVEDAY: Oh, but you both must. Listen. The reason I spilt the coffee
was that he had put poison in it!

MINISTER
DUCHESS: } (*Incredulous*) Poison? Poison!

LOVEDAY: Yes, poison. A deadly, secret poison, made from the karaka
nut. It would never have been detected, never! A few hours later

you would just have had a stroke and died! Of course he knows how dreadfully important you are.

MINISTER  } Bless my soul. Are you raving or am I dreaming,
DUCHESS:  } young lady. How do you know this—this amazing
          } thing? Fiddlesticks—tush—but, good God.

LOVEDAY: I saw him do it.

VARLIE-CHAPMAN: (*Putting on a superior air*) Can you really even *listen* to such an absurd charge against one of my cloth?

LOVEDAY: I can prove it. You will find on him a green carved jade hei-tiki, it has a secret recess in which the poison was. It must be on him. He couldn't swallow it, it's too big. Search him!

VARLIE-CHAPMAN: (*Calmly*) Search me, officer—if you are an officer—to satisfy the hysterical young lady and settle this absurd business once and for all.

LOVEDAY: Don't trust him. Have another man in to help. I charge him with attempted murder you know, murder of the most important Cabinet Minister.

DUCHESS: Oh, Loveday, this is too awful (*She sits*)

MINISTER: I feel a bit shaken, perhaps I may sit too.

SMITHERS: This is serious you know. It had better be looked into if you'll excuse me, sir. I have some of my men outside. If you would ring three times quickly, and then twice more, my men will come in. (*Loveday rushes to the bell and does so*) Thank you, Miss.

VARLIE: Waal, if this isn't high comedy! But *most* unseemly! And to think that it is in *your* house, Duchess, that I should be served up with this nice little surprise party.

(*Enter two stalwart plain clothes men from door on right*)

SMITHERS: Hold this gentleman firmly while we search his pockets. Excuse me, sir, but I think I ought to satisfy myself.

DUCHESS: I'm terribly distressed. I don't know what to think. I have known Loveday since she was six and had freckles on her nose, and she has *never* been hysterical.

LOVEDAY: (*Quietly*) I'm not hysterical now there are two such nice strong men to hold Mr. Varlie.

MINISTER: (*Pathetically*) *Could* I have some coffee do you think, my dear? I was really needing it before—

DUCHESS: Of course. This awful fracas must have exhausted you.

MINISTER: (*Shaking his finger playfully at her*) No fancy cakes now!

DUCHESS: There are none in my house, not even tonight. I may not be clever, but I can see the obvious as well as most people, and it is glaringly obvious that anyone whose hands are steady enough to decorate foodstuffs can handle tools of more use to the country. (*To* MAID *by curtains*) Go and fetch some hot coffee at once. I will stay by the curtains while you are gone. Don't say one word to anyone, mind!

(*She goes out quickly through door right. Meanwhile* SMITHERS *systematically searches all* VARLIE's *pockets. He finds a revolver, which he lays out with an accusing look*)

SMITHERS: That don't look like a clergyman, sir!

VARLIE: All Americans have those little pets on them. In the backwoods I have had to have it cocked on to my congregation so as to hold their attention!

(*Meanwhile* LOVEDAY *is quite quietly and unobtrusively looking round the corner, front right, where* VARLIE *had been standing before his arrest. The coffee comes in, the* MINISTER *drinks it, the* DUCHESS *returns from the curtains and the* MAID *takes up her place there again*)

MINISTER: This is very painful, my dear, very painful. I'm sure I don't know what to think.

DUCHESS: We must wait and see.

VARLIE: Waal, Duchess, in a time like the present I quite understand your young girls getting hysterical. Don't let my position make you feel bad. I bear no malice. It is my duty and my pleasure to turn the other cheek!

(LOVEDAY *stands gazing curiously at the palm, down right, near where* VARLIE *was. The smooth green moss is broken through in one place, and rough earth shows*)

SMITHERS: (*Rising*) There is no jade ornament too large for him to swallow on him that I can see.

VARLIE: Naturally! It grieves me that you should be so inured to deception, young man, that you should doubt my word.

MINISTER: There, there. It was all a fancy. But you and I and the Duchess can forgive a pretty girl more than this, can't we, Mr., Mr.—

VARLIE: Dr. Chapman, sir. Now your myrmidons can unhand me, I reckon.

(SMITHERS *hesitates to give the order*)

LOVEDAY: Don't! It's not settled. Look at this.

(SMITHERS *comes forward and looks at pot as she indicates*)

SMITHERS: I see nothing there, Miss.

LOVEDAY: The earth has been disturbed here—look, the rest of the pot is covered with moss.

DUCHESS: Oh, Loveday, Loveday. The gardener has pulled up a weed, I suppose. Pulling up weeds always does disturb the moss. Even the Government knows that.

LOVEDAY: Gordon, Mr. Smithers—haven't you a penknife one of you? Dig just there for me, please do.

VARLIE: (*Gets suddenly restive in his keepers' hands*) This is the limit! This beats everything. She put it there herself.

SMITHERS: (*Looking at him keenly*) Put it there? You said there wasn't anything just now.

VARLIE: I have had enough of this. (*To the two holding him*) Let me go, you monkey-faced jumbos. (*To* SMITHERS) I'm due at our Embassy. You can do your agricultural work as well when I've gone.

SMITHERS: (*Now suspicious of him*) We'll just see first if there is anything in this plant.

VARLIE: She did it herself. She simply put something in herself!

LOVEDAY: (*Spreading out her hands*) Look! I've got white kid gloves on! I *couldn't* have done it without leaving earth on them! and there isn't a grain!

MINISTER: (*Leans forward intently interested*) She is a bright girl that. I call that clever.

DUCHESS: Clever, yes. But not witty! She lost an opportunity of saying, "I have the proof at my finger tips."

MINISTER: (*Chuckling*) No case! The white gloves of a Judge on circuit!

DUCHESS: Good! Ha, ha!

LOVEDAY: Look at *his* hands. Look!

(VARLIE *closes his hands (which are gloveless) and clenches his nails in*)

VARLIE: By gum, you don't insult me like this!

SMITHERS: Please open your hands, sir.

VARLIE: I won't, damn you.

SMITHERS: You had better, sir.

VARLIE: I dropped a coin in a flower bed this afternoon! I have some earth in my nails anyway. (*He half opens his hands reluctantly*)

(ALL *lean forward to see. Two fingers are stained and there is earth in two or three of the nails*)

SMITHERS: You'd have washed your hands if what you say about dropping a coin is true before coming here, sir. Hold him well, men. Yes, Miss. I'll dig this pot up for you.

(*He digs with his penknife, all wait breathlessly, in a minute the green jade ornament appears. He wipes it with his handkerchief, holds it out to* LOVEDAY)

SMITHERS: Is that it, Miss.

LOVEDAY: (*Eager*) Yes, yes, that *is* it!

MINISTER ⎫ (*Coming forward to look at it*) Dear, dear! Fancy!
DUCHESS: ⎭ I said Loveday wasn't hysterical.

SMITHERS: That looks as though the young lady was right. You've had a narrow escape, sir!

VARLIE: That don't amount to shucks! What does that prove. There is only wild talk. I tell you I'm known at the American Embassy, I'm known to the Duchess here. You can't begin to prove I ever saw that green trumpery. The only thing you've got against me is that I wore a false beard! (*Sneers*) Bring that up against an American citizen and a minister of religion and you would look queer in the Law Courts!

LOVEDAY: And you are known to me—to us. To both Mr. Hyde and me. You were Mr. Varlie in New Zealand.

GORDON: Yes, Varlie, there's no mistaking you! You bought the freehold of my Station and all my sheep and I'm not likely to forget it.

LOVEDAY: And you travelled all over New Zealand, selling things under the name of Varlie, and you wouldn't be pretending to be somebody else and a clergyman too, if you were honest. Besides (*scornfully*), I saw you buy that special secret poison from Roto, the old Maori, and you made very special enquiries about its use, too!

SMITHERS: (*As though recollecting something*) Varlie—Varlie—New Zealand. The secret service particular warned me against a man called Varlie who has been hauling in a lot of freehold in New Zealand under various names, and travelling for German American firms. We had lost track of him. (*Joy spreading over his face*) You don't mean to say he is John Varlie! Not John Varlie, Miss?

LOVEDAY: Yes, yes.

GORDON: That's the name I've known him under in New Zealand for months.

SMITHERS: My, men! We have got a haul. Well, ladies, the man is safe now, anyway. There is no need to bother you any more tonight.

DUCHESS: Cleverness seems to get an appropriately solid result, Loveday?

SMITHERS: You are staying here, Miss? No? Your address, please.

(*He takes out a note book, she tells her address [a mumble and dumb show]*) And yours, sir? (GORDON *does the same*)

(*Meanwhile the* MINISTER *looks from one to the other, turns to* DUCHESS)

MINISTER: He is evidently really a dangerous man! But a *clergyman* too! What an outrage to the cloth. That's the kind of thing to make atheists.

SMITHERS: (*Snapping his note book and turning quickly*) He is no clergyman. A *very* dangerous man, sir. It is all a pretence too about his being an American. He is an out and out German, sir, and I make no doubt the young lady was right about his attempt on your life, sir. I expect you have had a narrow escape. We won't trouble you any further tonight. Take him off, men. I've got all the addresses. Good-night, ladies—good-night, sir, good-night, sir.

(*Goes out after* VARLIE, *led by the men, unresisting now*)

(LOVEDAY *and* GORDON *look at each other.* DUCHESS *subsides into sofa by the* MINISTER)

DUCHESS: As I said, even London is an adventure for the right man. (*Fans herself*) Loveday, come here.

MINISTER: (*Rises and shakes her hand, keeps it and pats it*) My dear young lady, my dear young lady. The service you have done me is too great for thanks. You may command me—always. And I hope I may often have the happiness of serving you. But please give me something to do at once. What can I do for you?

LOVEDAY: Oh, there *is* one thing you can do for me, if only you will! Will you!

MINISTER: An-y-thing you like to ask, my dear, if it is humanly possible. What is it?

LOVEDAY: Please, oh please, let Mr. Hyde tell you about his wonderful International plan.

MINISTER: Of course, of course! So he is a friend of yours, is he?

GORDON: (*Coming forward*) I have that great honour, sir.

GORDON: (*Takes out sheaf of papers*) If there was a Super-Parliament constituted as I suggest Prussian Militarism, all Militarism, is not only defeated now, but for ever! It is plucked out by the roots, but not at the ruinous cost of imposing militarism on all other nations. Oh, there's so much. (*Hesitates*)

LOVEDAY: (*Breaking in, her voice almost chanting, like one inspired, its notes resembling those used by her at the close of Act I*) And Militarism is met, not by the weakness of a too trusting idealism but by force controlled by intelligence. Law is devised with behind it international force, which shall protect the nations, as law backed by civil force protects each man and woman in Britain.

(HYDE *starts, gazing intently at her set inspired face and seems to recognise her voice. He stretches out a hand, withdraws it, and whispers in awed voice*)

HYDE: My queen! My vision. It is *she*! (*Sits as though entranced*)

LOVEDAY: (*Does not notice him, but continues uninterruptedly*) And the nation which will not come into this council of nations proclaims itself an outlaw, an aggressor, a planner of evil, and it inscribes its own doom, for law that is outraged takes vengeance implacable.

(*There is a pause, she relaxes—smiles*)

MINISTER: My dear—I must think.

LOVEDAY: (*Holding out her hands to him appealingly*) You are the most powerful man in England, it is for you to initiate this new era, of international safety and peace. Whatever the terms of an ordinary peace, militarism will spring up again to ravage the world. Let Britain lead in this new enlargement of law and freedom, for this is the only way to bring *security* to the world.

MINISTER: (*Very seriously*) I will think about it, my dear.

DUCHESS: (*Returning to her normal*) If that is cleverness it makes me a little dissatisfied with mere wit.

MINISTER: (*To* HYDE) Have your suggested constitution typed out, young man, and bring it to Downing Street the day after tomorrow. I'll send you a card with the hour. Your address? (HYDE *hands him a card*) I'll try to get the Prime Minister interested. Good-night.

LOVEDAY: How splendid.

MINISTER: Good-night, my dear, good-night. If you leave it very long before I see you again, I'll have to send for you. Heaven guard you, my dear.

(*To* DUCHESS) I must say good-night. I have long outstayed my time.

DUCHESS: Let me see you off my premises. I only pray there are no more adventures for you on them. I hope exterminated dangers leave rest behind them. (*They go off back centre together, the* FOOTMAN *pulls curtain apart to let them out and follows them. Faint strains of music are heard from distant room*)

LOVEDAY: (*Sits on sofa, looks at* GORDON *with a rapt gaze*) Your chance, the world's chance, has come!

GORDON: (*In awe-struck voice, tenderly. He stands half stooping before her*) And *you*, you are not only my friend but my Goddess, my vision! Your look just now—your wonderful voice when you were speaking to the Minister a little ago. It was you that night in the woods—you I have been adoring, and from you I have been drawing my inspiration!

LOVEDAY: (*Softly*) It was I in the woods. Chance gave me a moment's inspiration! which you worked into reality.

GORDON: (*Half kneels before her*) I know my love can be nothing at all to you—I am not a fit mate for you. But let me go on kneeling to you! Don't spurn me.

LOVEDAY: (*Slowly*) Why are you so sure your love is nothing to me?

GORDON: (*As though blinded by a sudden shaft of light in the darkness*) Oh! It can't be that it *is* anything to you?

LOVEDAY: Your love is everything to me.

(*Slowly he advances, with almost incredulous rapture. They kiss*)

CURTAIN

# A Note About the Author

Marie Stopes (1880–1958) was a British author, activist, eugenicist, and paleobotanist. Born in Edinburgh, Scotland, Stopes was the daughter of Henry Stopes, a paleontologist, and Charlotte Carmichael Stopes, a women's rights activist and Shakespearean scholar. Raised in London, she attended meetings of the British Association for the Advancement of Science from a young age, eventually enrolling at University College London to study botany and geology. In 1902, the year of her graduation, she began working with Dr. Francis Oliver as a research assistant. After participating in a groundbreaking discovery of fossil specimens containing intact fern fronds and seeds, Stopes completed her D. Sc., making her the youngest Briton in history to attain the degree. Her own research focused on Carboniferous coal balls from throughout different geological eras, but she eventually turned away from paleobotany to focus on the issue of birth control. In 1913, after meeting Margaret Sanger, and spurred on by her impending divorce, Stopes published *Married Love or Love in Marriage*, a guide for couples intended to promote birth control and foster healthy sexual relationships. Working with husband Humphrey Roe, Stopes founded the first birth control clinic in Britain in 1921, offering free services for married women in need of contraceptives and sexual education. Like many of her contemporaries, Stopes opposed abortion and was an ardent supporter of eugenics, even entrusting her clinic to the Eugenics Society after her death from breast cancer at the age of 77.

# A Note from the Publisher

Spanning many genres, from non-fiction essays to literature classics to children's books and lyric poetry, Mint Edition books showcase the master works of our time in a modern new package. The text is freshly typeset, is clean and easy to read, and features a new note about the author in each volume. Many books also include exclusive new introductory material. Every book boasts a striking new cover, which makes it as appropriate for collecting as it is for gift giving. Mint Edition books are only printed when a reader orders them, so natural resources are not wasted. We're proud that our books are never manufactured in excess and exist only in the exact quantity they need to be read and enjoyed.

# bookfinity™

## Discover more of your favorite classics with Bookfinity™.

- Track your reading with custom book lists.
- Get great book recommendations for your personalized Reader Type.
- Add reviews for your favorite books.
- AND MUCH MORE!

Visit **bookfinity.com** and take the fun Reader Type quiz to get started.

Enjoy our classic and modern companion pairings!

## Classic & Modern